THE
MOUNTIES

Tales of Adventure and Danger from the Early Days

ELLE ANDRA-WARNER

VICTORIA · VANCOUVER · CALGARY

Heritage House Publishing Company Ltd.
#108 – 17665 66A Avenue
Surrey, BC V3S 2A7
www.heritagehouse.ca

Heritage House Publishing Company Ltd.
PO Box 468
Custer, WA
98240-0468

Library and Archives Canada Cataloguing in Publication
Andra-Warner, Elle, 1946-
  The Mounties: tales of adventure and danger from the early days / Elle Andra-Warner.—1st Heritage House ed.

Includes bibliographical references.
ISBN 978-1-894974-67-7

  1. North West Mounted Police (Canada)—History. 2. Royal North West Mounted Police (Canada)—History. 3. Royal Canadian Mounted Police—History. 4. Northwest, Canadian—History—1870–1905. I. Title.

FC3216.2.A54 2009   971.2'02   C2008-908134-X

Originally published 2004 by Altitude Publishing Canada Ltd.

Library of Congress Control Number: 209920310

Series editor: Lesley Reynolds.
Cover design: Chyla Cardinal. Interior design: Frances Hunter.
Cover photo courtesy of John Woodruff. Interior photos by Don Boone, page 20; Glenbow Archives, page 28 (NA-3173-9), page 43 (NA-784-1), page 67 (NA-919-15), and page 74 (NA-2615-11); and Yukon Archives, page 31 (#4686).

 Mixed Sources
Cert no. SW-COC-001271
© 1996 FSC
FSC   The interior of this book was printed on 100% post-consumer recycled paper, processed chlorine free and printed with vegetable-based inks.

Heritage House acknowledges the financial support for its publishing program from the Government of Canada through the Book Publishing Industry Development Program (BPIDP), Canada Council for the Arts and the province of British Columbia through the British Columbia Arts Council and the Book Publishing Tax Credit.

BRITISH COLUMBIA
ARTS COUNCIL   The Canada Council | Le Conseil des Arts
for the Arts | du Canada

12 11 10 09   1 2 3 4 5

Printed in Canada

For my daughter Cindi

Contents

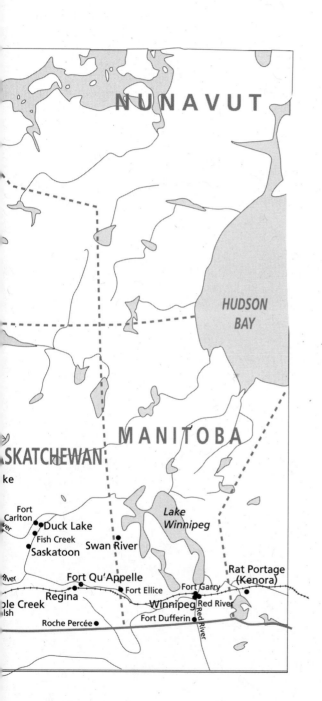

Prologue

FOR THREE DAYS, A RAGING *blizzard had forced the two RCMP officers and their guide to stay in their igloo on Bathurst Island. It was the winter of 1929, and Inspector A.H. Joy and Constable R.A. Taggart were on a historic 2,700-kilometre, 81-day patrol through the Arctic's Parry Islands.*

On the third night, as the men were sleeping, their leashed sled dogs suddenly began to bark ferociously. Joy looked outside and saw that there was a huge polar bear within their camp area. Usually the dogs' barking would scare the polar bears away. Usually, but not on that night.

The polar bear approached the group's supply sled and began to claw at the covering. Watching from the igloo, Joy asked the others to give him the loaded rifle. It was then that the men realized their rifle—their one and only firearm—was sitting outside the igloo by the snow-packed entrance. Quickly the threesome started to clear the blocked entrance with their snow knives, but their frantic voices brought the curious bear to the igloo. The animal charged at the blocked passageway, trying to get through.

Shouting and screaming all the while, the men finally cut a hole through the packed snow close to the rifle. But the bear saw them and again lunged at the igloo's entrance, trying to squeeze inside. The men slashed at the bear with their snow knives, and Taggart swung a club at the animal, hitting hard on the tip of its nose. Snarling, the bear backed away. At that moment, Taggart tried to reach the rifle, but the bear saw him and attacked, forcing him back into the igloo.

Again Taggart hit the bear's nose, and again the bear withdrew. Quickly, Taggart grabbed for the rifle, but held it for only a second before the bear knocked the weapon from his hand. Once again he was forced to fall back. The angry bear then hurled itself at the opening, got partly in and became stuck. Fighting for their lives, the terrified men kicked and pummelled the bear until finally it retreated into the clearing. Then it stood up and glared at the igloo. Seizing the moment, Taggart crawled out with lightning speed and snatched the rifle leaning near the entrance. With one shot, he killed the bear.

CHAPTER

1

How It All Began

IT WAS ONE OF THE greatest real estate deals of all time. On July 15, 1870, the Dominion of Canada finally owned all of Canada. It had paid £300,000 and land grants to the Hudson's Bay Company (HBC) to buy control of Rupert's Land—a huge chunk of property equivalent to almost 40 percent of modern-day Canada. This area included all of today's Manitoba, Saskatchewan, Alberta, Yukon, Northwest Territories and Nunavut, as well as large portions of Quebec and Ontario.

The vast region had been ruled by the HBC for over 200 years—ever since the Royal Charter of May 2, 1670, when England's King Charles II had granted a group of 18 English investors the "sole possession of all the seas, waters, lakes, and lands of the Hudson Bay and the drainage system." The grant had given the HBC absolute powers over the land, including the right to create and enforce laws, have its own army and navy, and make peace or war with the Natives. While the HBC had controlled the land, it had maintained law through justices of the peace located at the fur-trading posts and a court system (both for criminal and civil cases) in Fort Garry.

Rupert's Land, which had been named for Prince Rupert, the cousin of King Charles II, stretched more than five million square kilometres. And now it all belonged to Canada.

But there was a problem: its southwest prairies were wild and lawless—so dangerous that some areas could only be travelled with an armed escort. Warring Native tribes, rogue hunters and unscrupulous traders roamed the land, unwilling to recognize the international boundary. Many lived by the gun, defying both American and Canadian laws.

The most notorious scoundrels were the Americans who were crossing into Canada to illegally trade guns and homemade whisky to the Natives in exchange for buffalo robes and furs. The whisky, commonly known as "firewater," was a wicked mixture of pure alcohol, water, tobacco juice, ginger and molasses. One or two cupfuls would be traded for a buffalo hide. The liquor was destroying the Native people and wiping out the buffalo herds, which were being indiscriminately hunted not for food, but for hides to be used as trade goods.

These American whisky traders set up a series of trading forts or posts across the Prairies, reaching as far north as present-day Edmonton. Most of the posts were small and cabin-like and were only used for a season or two. When their legitimacy was challenged by the men of the HBC, the traders said they would do as they pleased, as there was no police force to stop them, and then kept on selling their firewater.

The largest and most profitable of the whisky trading posts was Fort Whoop-Up, located at the foothills of the Rockies about 60 kilometres north of the Canada–United States border, a few kilometres south of present-day Lethbridge, Alberta. Fort Whoop-Up belonged to whisky merchants Alfred Baker Hamilton, John Jerome Healy and Healy's brother Thomas, all from Fort Benton, Montana, which was just across the border on the Missouri River.

The primary purpose of Fort Whoop-Up was to make a quick profit by trading contraband whisky to Native peoples in the unprotected southern Canadian prairies. However, other goods were also traded. These goods were supplied by T.C. Power Company in Fort Benton and brought into Canada by bull wagons that took 10 to 12 days' travel time. They included items like tobacco, guns, blankets, cloth, sugar, canned goods and mirrors. Still, the fort was best known for its illegal whisky. The wicked concoction was nicknamed "Whoop-Up Bug Juice" and was comprised of whisky, chewing tobacco, red pepper, Jamaica ginger and molasses. These ingredients were diluted with water and heated to the boiling point. Whoop-Up Bug Juice was traded by the cupful or by the keg to the Natives who, not understanding the dangers of firewater, would get drunk and became violent, sometimes killing each other outside the walls of the fort.

It was the drunken wrath of some Blood First Nations that burned and destroyed the original Fort Whoop-Up (11 log huts constructed in 1869) in its first year. But the Americans quickly rebuilt it in 1870, heavily fortifying it to withstand a future attack. The second Whoop-Up was a palisaded fortress. It measured 39 by 42 metres, with a 5-metre-tall oak gate and heavy-timbered, mud-chinked walls with loopholes for guns and muskets. Two bastions (blockhouses) with mounted three-pounder guns were located at opposite corners, offset from the walls. One cannon was positioned so that it could be fired at anyone attempting to break through the gate, and the other was aimed straight at the gate in case an uninvited guest entered. Inside the log walls were storerooms, living quarters, a kitchen, a blacksmith shop and stables. The roof was made of logs and then covered with sod to prevent Native peoples in the area from setting the fort on fire by shooting flaming arrows. The chimneys were crossed with iron bars for protection.

Because of past incidents of whisky-induced violence, Natives were forbidden inside the fort. When they came to trade, they pushed their buffalo robes to a trader through a small wicket-like opening in the wall; the trader then handed them the tin cupfuls of whisky in return.

The Canadian government realized the whisky trade was having disastrous effects on the Native peoples of the Prairies and knew it had to be eliminated. The violence and lack of law and order were obstacles to the government's plan to quickly settle the Canadian West with European immigrant homesteaders. Government officials were also concerned that if they didn't develop a strong Canadian presence in their newly acquired western lands, the Americans might further encroach on Canada and perhaps even try to annex it from the British Empire. Moreover, Canada's sovereignty would be at risk if the American government ordered the US Cavalry to cross the boundary line to start policing the Canadian southwest and they found no Canadian force to stop them.

Prime Minister Sir John A. Macdonald began planning how best to deliver law, order and stability to the Canadian West. He envisioned a constabulary police force of mounted riflemen modelled after the Royal Irish Constabulary (RIC) and India's Bengal Mounted Police. Both forces were centrally controlled by a civilian administration, unlike local police forces. Macdonald liked the concept of a government-legislated force, which would make the police direct representatives of Her Majesty.

But it wasn't until May 3, 1873, that Macdonald introduced a bill to the Canadian Parliament calling for the establishment of a force of mounted riflemen, identified simply as a "Police Force for the North-West Territories."

(North-West Territories was the name given to Rupert's Land, excluding the Red River settlement region, which became the province of Manitoba and joined the Dominion of Canada in 1870.) Though the bill passed unanimously, no further government action was taken to start recruitment for some time.

The catalyst for fast-tracking the mounted police into reality was a cold-blooded spring massacre on the Prairies.

The Cypress Hills Massacre

It began in late May 1873, when an unruly group of wolfers (wolf hunters who used poisoned buffalo meat as bait) left Fort Benton, Montana, and crossed the 49th parallel boundary line into Canada in pursuit of Cree who had allegedly stolen some of their horses. Led by Civil War veteran John H. Evans and ex-Confederate Army soldier Thomas Hardwick, the posse was bent on revenge as they followed the stolen horses' tracks to Cypress Hills, 60 kilometres north of the Canadian-American boundary in today's southwestern Saskatchewan.

The area, which was a traditional camping ground for Native peoples, had also become a centre for whisky traders like American Abel Farwell and German-born Moses Solomon. The two men had built their trading posts— Farwell's Fort and Solomon's Post—almost directly across from each other on a tributary of the Milk River now called Battle Creek. Farwell, a tall, heavyset man, was more popular with the Native people in the area, as he had married a Cree woman named Mary Horseguard. She worked alongside him as his partner, along with New Brunswick–born George Hammond.

The Benton wolfers dropped into Farwell's Fort for some drinking. When they heard that about 200 Assiniboine were camped on a flat piece of prairie along the creek across from Farwell's Fort and to the east of Solomon's Post, they shifted their anger with the Cree onto the nearby Native camp and started making attack plans. Some accounts report that they sent the Assiniboine a "complimentary" keg of liquor to get them drunk and make them easier to kill.

Farwell told the Benton gang that the Assiniboine had not stolen their horses, but he could see it didn't matter one bit what he said—the wolfers were intent on killing. According to some accounts, Farwell then tried to prevent the violence by going to meet with the Assiniboine leader, Little Soldier. While the two men were talking, the wolfers arrived and called out for Farwell to get out of the way. Farwell shouted back that if they fired, he would fight with the Natives. He asked the Benton gang to hold off on taking any action until he went back to his fort to fetch his interpreter, Alexis LeBombard, to mediate. But as he raced to the post, the first shots rang out and the killing began.

Some stories claim that Little Soldier tried to rouse his warriors, many of who were drunk or asleep. But it was too late. The posse murdered Little Soldier, cut off his head and mounted it on a long pole. They then went on to slaughter men, women and children, even shooting elders who were hiding in the creek bed. The Assiniboine could not stop the carnage. As the survivors scrambled to take refuge in the hills and make their way to safety at a nearby Métis camp, the wolfers captured several terrified women and assaulted them.

At daybreak, the wolfers pillaged and then set fire to the camp. It was a horrible sight: dead bodies scattered among the burning lodges and Little Soldier's head still on a lodge pole high above the camp. Over 30 Assiniboine, innocent of horse theft, had been brutally massacred.

The wolfers, meanwhile, had lost only one man in the massacre: a Canadian named Ed Grace, who died after being shot by an arrow. Farwell and Solomon, fearing for their lives, loaded their wagons and hastily abandoned their whisky posts before both posts were burned.

News of the Cypress Hills Massacre didn't reach the Canadian government until early September, mere days after Prime Minister Macdonald had signed an order-in-council, dated August 30, that launched the "Police Force for the North-West." The Force soon became known as the North-West Mounted Police (NWMP), although it wouldn't officially be given that title until 1879.

The massacre pushed the government to bring the mounted police into existence all the more quickly. On September 25, 1873, an order-in-council appointed nine commissioned officers to the new mounted force. Their job was to immediately begin recruitment of 150 men and, before winter, to get them to Stone Fort, also known as HBC's Lower Fort Garry. It was called Stone Fort by the First Nations of the area, and this became the name used by the Mounties.

Mountie Politics

Recruiting posters were widely posted, calling for men "of sound constitution, active and able-bodied, able to ride, of good character, able to read and write either the English or French language, and between the ages of 18 and 40 years." The original term of service was three years, after which time members would be eligible for a land grant of 160 acres in the North-West Territories (this offer was later rescinded).

The Force was set up as a paramilitary body, divided into troops and headed by a commissioner. Pay was dismal: 75 cents per day for sub-constables, $1 for constables, $400 to $600 per year for veterinary surgeons, $1,000 to $1,400 per year for superintendents and surgeons, and $2,000 to $2,600 per year for commissioners. But despite the feeble salaries, the NWMP appealed to those with a spirit and thirst for adventure. One young recruit later wrote that he thought life in the NWMP would be "one grand round of riding wild mustangs, chasing whisky traders and horse thieves ... and meeting lovely, sophisticated Princesses ..."

A memorial to the North-West Mounted Police in Collingwood, Ontario.

Legislation allowed for an authorized strength of 300 men, but the government felt 150 was a sufficient number to police the sparsely populated West. Thousands of men applied when recruitment began in September 1873 at centres in Ontario, Quebec and the Maritimes. In Toronto alone there were 622 applicants for 50 vacancies.

The successful candidates were divided into three troops of 50 men—Troops A, B and C. It was a diverse group that included 9 farmers, 46 clerks, 13 police or military men, 43 skilled workers and 39 listed as "miscellaneous or no previous experience."

The first commissioner of the NWMP was Lieutenant Colonel George Arthur French, a gunner born in Roscommon, Ireland, and educated in the British military. He had come to Canada in 1871 as a military inspector at the request of the Canadian government, became the head of the School of Gunnery in Kingston and in 1873 was appointed to organize the NWMP. (He resigned in 1876, returned to duty in the British Army and received a knighthood when he retired in 1902. For the next 19 years until he died in 1921, he guarded the crown jewels in London, England.)

The First Trek

In early October 1873, the men assembled at the Collingwood docks on Lake Huron to sail 875 kilometres by steamer to Prince Arthur's Landing (later renamed Port Arthur, now part of the City of Thunder Bay) on the western shores of Lake Superior. From there, they would travel almost 700 kilometres to Stone Fort, south of today's Winnipeg. It was a gruelling, unpredictable overland route through forests, lakes, rivers, swamps and steep terrain blocked by tree roots and ancient boulders.

Simon J. Dawson first surveyed the route in 1858. Ten years later, the government ordered him back to build the route as a trail for immigrant settlers headed west. Named the Dawson Route, it was known as the only "all-Canadian" route to the North-West (though it briefly dipped three times into the United States). Dawson told travellers they could journey the route from Thunder Bay to North West Angle on Lake of the Woods in as little as six days.

In 1870, during the Red River Rebellion, an expedition led by Colonel John Garnet Wolseley and consisting of 1,200 soldiers (both Canadian militia and British troops) had used the Dawson Route when they were sent to Manitoba to restore order. The expedition had included future NWMP leaders like Sam Steele, James Walsh and James Macleod. It had been a brutal journey on the newly opened route, one that had involved road building, navigating, poling, tracking and tackling over 40 difficult portages.

Now, three years later, Steele, Macleod and Walsh would again trek on the difficult Dawson Route to Manitoba.

Arriving in the West

The first of the new mounted police force—an advance party consisting of 33-year-old Inspector James Walsh and 40 men of Troop A—left Collingwood on October 4 aboard the paddlewheel steamer *Cumberland*. Before the steamer left the dock, the following order was given to the troops: "The C.O. [Commissioning Officer] requests that the men will abstain from too free use of intoxicating liquors. While he is no advocate for totally abstaining still it will be his duty to report to the Commissioner on his arrival at Stone Fort any cases of drunkenness that may be brought before him."

On October 10, the second group, consisting of the two officers and 62 men of Troop B, left Collingwood on the famous SS *Chicora*, a historic ship built at Liverpool in 1864 as the Confederate blockade runner *Let Her Be*. Purchased by a Canadian and brought to the Great Lakes in 1868, she was cut in two to pass through the St. Lawrence locks and Welland Canal. The ship was reassembled at Buffalo to operate as a first-class passenger boat and renamed *Chicora*.

After a stormy passage on Lake Superior, the second group arrived at Prince Arthur's Landing, where it joined the advance group and together started down the Dawson Route on three-horse wagons. With excellent fall weather they made good travelling time, arriving at Stone Fort on October 22.

The last contingent of 53 men, Troop C, under officers Young, Brennan and James Macleod (the future NWMP commissioner), left Collingwood on the steamer *Frances Smith* late at night on October 10. From the beginning, they were plagued with terrible weather and bad luck. The *Frances Smith* ran into a severe snowstorm on Lake Superior. It was reported that the crossing was one of the roughest in four years, leaving everyone violently seasick, except for Inspector Macleod. After arriving at Prince Arthur's Landing, the group loaded up the wagons to travel the 77-kilometre road to Lake Shebandowan. From there, they would row, sail, pole and portage the remaining 600 kilometres to Stone Fort.

The Dawson Route had several "stopping houses" where travellers could stop for food (meals were 30 cents) and replenish their supplies—just as Troop C of the NWMP planned to do. Unfortunately, by the time this group set out on the trail, the stopover houses were empty; the road authorities had pulled their men and closed the route for the winter, as they thought all the NWMP troops had already travelled by.

It was now late October with winter settling in, and it appeared the men of Troop C would have to travel hundreds of kilometres without provisions or places to resupply until the HBC's Fort Frances, located almost 300 kilometres away on the shores of Rainy Lake and Rainy River (geographically situated on the Ontario-Minnesota border). The officers decided there would be no turning back, they would continue west and take their chances.

Along the route they broke into every stopping house, trying to find food. Hungry and tired, they ran into winter's early snow as they reached the international waters of Rainy Lake. Boats piloted by Iroquois crews met the men to transport them to Fort Frances, but the Iroquois had no food provisions for them.

Though disappointed, the men were eager to arrive at Fort Frances, where they would finally be able to purchase food and supplies—or so they thought. Major J.G. Bray of Troop C wrote what happened next: "The moment we landed, the late Sergeant Parker and myself went for the Hudson's Bay post; the postmaster civilly opened the store for us and asked us first if we were Mounted Police and what we wanted. We told him everything he had in the store for supper for seventy men. He told us he was 'exceedingly sorry' that he had nothing a white man could use except two barrels of cube sugar, that he hadn't a pound of flour or an ounce of meat for his own family."

Disheartened, the men spent the night on the snow-covered beach, wearing their summer clothes and no winter boots. None of them had warm overcoats or blankets. The only food for breakfast was the dried apples they had taken from a stopping house. Hungry and cold, the next day they ran the 3-kilometre Meline Rapids to reach Rainy River, a 130-kilometre-long river that connects Rainy Lake and Lake of the Woods.

Their luck briefly changed for the better when they later landed on the American side of the Rainy River and found a nearby Chippewa camp with an abundance of white fish and corn. The Chippewa were readying their food for the winter, but stopped to prepare a generous meal of boiled fish and corn for the starving NWMP.

After camping beside the Chippewa for the night, Troop C headed out the next morning, but terrible weather followed them again. As they reached the mouth of Lake of the Woods, where a steamboat was waiting for them, a violent snowstorm delayed their departure for three days. When they finally sailed across Lake of the Woods to North West Angle, they had to break ice for 45 metres just to get to shore.

Once they arrived at North West Angle they were only 160 kilometres away from Fort Garry. As Bray wrote, "At this point we found two conveyances—one a covered cart for the officers, and the other one a 'Red River' cart loaded with government tents; but [the tents] were not available for us because they were frozen hard. We took the carts with us, and got two meals in about 4 days. Our last night was spent at Fort Lachine [now Oak Point] where we slept on the open prairie in a blizzard; next morning we started to march without anything to eat, in 10 below zero, for Fort Garry; our faces frozen in places, and some of our fingers and toes were frostbitten."

The men plodded 32 kilometres in bitter cold through deep snow. Their clothing gave them no protection and their boots froze solid. Some members of the troop wrapped their feet in underwear and shirts just to be able to keep on marching.

When Troop C finally arrived at Fort Garry, they were met by Bishop Tache, who insisted they spend the night in lodgings at St. Boniface Cathedral. (Bray called it "The Archbishop's Palace.") It was like heaven to the troops—hot food and clean sheets on their beds. But the next morning, the brief interlude with comfort was over, and the men headed back out into the freezing cold to journey to their winter headquarters at Stone Fort. To get there, they had to cross the recently frozen Red River, a dangerous undertaking. Left with no real alternative, each man carefully picked his way across the thin ice, one at a time, and they were all soon reunited with the two other troops.

On a cold and cloudy Monday morning, November 3, 1873, the men of the three divisions were sworn in as members of the Police Force of the North-West. After giving their oath, the non-commissioned men signed a paper promising three years of obedient service and to reimburse the government for any damage they might cause to its property. The officers received their commissions from Queen Victoria and did not need to sign.

The first non-commissioned officer to sign the oath was Arthur Henry Griesbach, a professional soldier and veteran of South Africa's Cape Mounted Rifles (his son William, at the age of 28, would become Edmonton's "boy mayor" in 1906); the second to sign was Percy Reginald Neale; and the third was a young man who would become one of the great legends in Mountie history, 24-year-old Samuel Benfield Steele.

The men were issued fatigue uniforms and arms and began training immediately. Steele was tasked with breaking the broncos (purchased out west) and instructing the men in riding. He later described this task in *Forty Years in Canada*: "Even when we had them 'gentled' so as to let recruits mount, the men were repeatedly thrown with great violence to the frozen ground, but no one lost his nerve ..."

The First Patrol

The first call for NWMP policing came in early December 1873. Word reached Stone Fort that whisky traders were selling liquor to Native peoples on the west coast of Lake

Constable Frederick A. Bagley at age 15.

Winnipeg. Commissioner French assigned Inspector James Macleod (soon to be assistant commissioner) to lead a patrol to immediately investigate and arrest the traders. Macleod selected four NWMP officers and guides to accompany him. After learning how to snowshoe, the patrol set off.

Initially, the five men travelled on horse-drawn sleighs with two dog teams that pulled toboggans loaded with a tent, blankets and food. Then, from the mouth of the

Red River, the men snowshoed and mushed for several days until they reached the log cabin headquarters of the whisky traders.

The patrol arrested six men, confiscated about 10 gallons of liquor and returned to Stone Fort with their prisoners on Christmas Eve. The first NWMP patrol had been a success.

The Second Contingent

During the winter of 1873–74, Commissioner French determined that the NWMP could effectively police the West, but only if Force numbers were doubled. By that time, Macdonald's government had fallen, so French went to Ottawa to convince Alexander Mackenzie, the new prime minister, of the urgent need for additional troops. Mackenzie finally agreed to the request, and French set about recruiting 150 men in Toronto for three new divisions (Troops D, E and F) to join the first contingent already training in Manitoba.

Recruits had to be 18 years of age, but 15-year-old Frederick "Fred" Augustus Bagley, an experienced horseman, went down to the NWMP recruiting office intent on enlisting anyway. On May 1, 1874, he wrote the following in his diary: "Colonel George Arthur French, the Commissioner of the Force, and my father had served together in the Royal Artillery of the British Imperial Army, and the Colonel at once informed my father, in down town Toronto of my action and whereabouts. Father lost no time in coming post haste to interview the Colonel, with the view of preventing my enlistment, but after a rather stormy argument between us he arranged with the Colonel to take me on as Trumpeter for a period of not more than six months. And so I am now a member of the N.W.M.P. at the age of fifteen years." (Bagley served with the NWMP for the next 25 years.)

On June 6, 1874, two special railway cars left Toronto heading west, carrying 217 NWMP (extra men had been hired, as some recruits were expected to desert) and 244 horses. At Sarnia they added nine railway cars of equipment, and at Detroit, two cars containing 34 more horses. The train route took them through the American cities of Chicago (where outlaw Jesse James' brother Frank was said to have watched them from his hotel, which was adjacent to where the NWMP kept their horses overnight) and St. Paul before arriving in Fargo, North Dakota, on June 12.

On June 13, the troops rode out on the five-day overland journey to Fort Dufferin near Pembina, North Dakota, where they would meet the first contingent of troops. It wasn't an easy journey—reveille was usually at 4 a.m. and marching started at 5 or 6 a.m. Men and horses were exhausted; some of the eastern horses died.

Meanwhile, the first contingent from Stone Fort had already ridden south to Fort Dufferin to wait for the three new troop divisions. When Troops D, E and F arrived on June 19, it was the first time the six NWMP troop divisions, totalling about 300 men, were together.

A uniformed member of the NWMP.

Prairie storms can be wicked, and the next night a vicious thunderstorm wreaked havoc on the combined campsite. Heavy rain pounded down as thunder boomed continuously and lighting sizzled in the sky. The intensity of the storm was so petrifying that the horses stampeded. Sam Steele wrote about the chaotic night in his memoirs: "A thunderbolt fell in the midst of the horses. Terrified, they broke their fastenings and made for the side of the

31

corral. The six men on guard were trampled underfoot as they tried to stop them. The maddened beasts overturned the huge wagons, dashed through a row of tents, scattered everything, and made for the gate of the large field in which we were camped ... they rushed the gate and attempted to pass it, scrambling and rolling over one another in one huge mass."

The spooked horses were crazed with fear. Steele recorded that the rolling thunder and pandemonium in the camp "gave to it a weird and romantic complexion, typically suggestive of the wild west."

Of the 300 horses, about 250 fled south over the Pembina bridge and continued for another 50 to 80 kilometres into North Dakota. A group of veteran riders, including Steele, covered over 160 kilometres in the next 24 hours searching for the runaway horses and successfully returned all but one. Young Bagley had ridden with the searchers; on their return he was so exhausted that he fell asleep in his saddle and had to be lifted off his horse—Old Buck—and put to bed.

Three weeks later, on July 9, 1874, the NWMP was on the move, headed west to find the notorious Fort Whoop-Up, the American trading centre for illegal whisky.

The March West

The story of the March West has been the subject of many books and films, yet no matter how many times it has been told, it remains a fascinating drama of endurance and hardship.

It was an impressive sight when the NWMP departed Fort Dufferin around 5 p.m. on July 9. The tight column stretched back more than 4 kilometres and consisted of 274 Mounties (including one surgeon and 11 veterinary surgeons), 20 Métis guides and 310 horses, followed by a collection of other animals and equipment that included 2 mortars, 2 one-ton cannons, 114 oxcarts, 73 wagons, 33 head of beef cattle, 142 work oxen, forges, mowing machines, farming equipment, ploughs and more.

It was a colourful spectacle as the column moved along. The Mounties wore their dress uniforms: scarlet jackets, tight-fitting grey breeches, pillbox caps or snow-white pith helmets, white gauntlet gloves and shining black boots. Each troop could be identified by the colour of its horses— dark bays for Troop A, dark browns for B, bright chestnuts for C, greys for D, blacks for E and light bays for F.

Indeed, the NWMP looked very organized as they marched away from Fort Dufferin. But in reality the march was poorly planned and the men were ill prepared. The scarlet wool tunics were impractical for prairie conditions; the horses from eastern Ontario were so unsuitable for long prairie treks and pulling wagons that they began to die; the rifles (Snider-Enfield Mark I single-shot carbine) were inferior to the repeating rifles owned by the Natives; and many of the first batch of revolvers had arrived damaged. As well,

Commissioner French had assumed there would be drink-able water along the way—there wasn't. Before long, both the men and the animals were desperate for water.

Even the route they took to reach Fort Whoop-Up spelled disaster. They could have taken the well-used fur trade trail between Red River and Fort Edmonton and then turned south to reach Fort Whoop-Up, or they could have followed the road made by the Boundary Commission sur-veying the western half of the Canada–United States border. But instead, Commissioner French and the North-West Territories lieutenant governor, Alexander Morris, mapped out a new route that would take the Mounties into unknown terrain, where water was either scarce or alkaline and the landscape was barren and dry.

Two days after leaving Fort Dufferin, Bagley wrote the following in his diary: "We had nothing to eat or drink from 6 a.m. until 9 p.m. ... Collected buckets of water by digging in mud."

The group travelled an average of 43 kilometres a day for the first few weeks, but then hot prairie weather began to take its toll and bouts of diarrhea became common among the men. Worse still, the weakening eastern horses con-cerned French so greatly that on July 22, he ordered the men to walk every second hour, regardless of whether they were riding a horse or a wagon. This resulted in another problem: with the men doing more walking, the leather of their rid-ing boots began to wear out.

On July 24, Bagley wrote, "Made about 11 miles [18 kilometres] in the afternoon and camped on the Souris River, near La Roche Percee [near today's Estevan]. My feet blistered and bleeding through walking in riding boots. Captain James Walker carried me pick a back [piggyback] for some distance into camp."

That same day, at the wind-carved limestone formations of Roche Percée, where there was plenty of water, pasture and wood, French allowed the men and animals to stop for a longer rest of five days. During that time, he strategized on how he could speed up the progress of the march. He decided the best course of action would be to lighten the load, removing the sick men and weak horses from the march and sending them to Fort Ellice. To do this, he would shift them to Troop A, along with the slow carts and cattle. At the same time, the best horses of Troop A would be distributed to the other divisions. French directed Inspector William D. Jarvis and Sergeant Sam Steele to lead the "new" Troop A to Fort Edmonton, first dropping off the worst cases at Fort Ellice and then continuing their journey on the northern route (Fort Carlton Trail) with the strongest men and animals. The makeshift group left Roche Percée on July 29 with the sick men, as well as 25 healthy men from Troop A, 12 Métis drivers/guides, 24 wagons and the weakest livestock (55 horses, 62 oxen and 50 cows and calves).

Meanwhile, the main group (now consisting of five divisions) continued southwest, following the route made two years earlier by the surveyors of the international boundary. In front were advance parties looking for water and grass for the animals. And stretching back almost 16 kilometres were the slower members on the wagons, as well as the cattle and oxen. Sometimes the slower men were so far behind that they failed to catch up with the main group in the evening for dinner, not that the meals were great—the staple diet was soggy bread, salt bacon and flapjacks fried in axle grease.

When the horses became too weak to carry any riders, the men walked. As the condition of the animals continued to deteriorate, the Mounties themselves had to hand-haul the wagons up the hills. By September they were still trekking. Often there would be no wood or dry buffalo chips for fire fuel, which meant there would be no supper. Everyone went to bed hungry and cold.

Another ongoing problem was the reliability of the guides, particularly an American scout named Morrow who had joined them along the march. French suspected that Morrow might be a spy sent by the whisky traders. In early September, Morrow led them to what he said was the confluence of the Bow and Belly Rivers. According to the scouts, this was where they would find Fort Whoop-Up. But when French looked closely at the river, he realized it was actually a sharp curve in the South Saskatchewan. French wrote in his diary on September 6: "There is not a soul in camp that knows this place." And it got worse. On

September 8, rainstorms and a cold north wind replaced the earlier prairie heat of summer. After five horses died on the night of September 9, French ordered each of the men to surrender one of their blankets to cover a horse at night. On September 10, sensing they were lost, Bagley noted in his diary: "The Commissioner and guides seem to be very hazy as to where we are. Everyone glum and low spirits. Future prospects gloom."

Finally, the scouts located the confluence of the Belly and Bow Rivers, but instead of the large fortified Fort Whoop-Up, they found only three broken-down, abandoned cabins. And the grazing land that was supposedly close to Fort Whoop-Up was nowhere to be seen.

French realized the seriousness of the situation—the men were demoralized, and quick action was needed to keep the animals from starving. He called for a meeting of his senior officers and told them that for the moment they would forget about Fort Whoop-Up and concentrate on getting the men and horses to safety. In the southern horizon he could see three buttes of the Sweet Grass Hills near the Montana border, and on September 15 the troops headed across the prairies towards them. The journey was exhausting for the men and animals alike, averaging only 25 kilometres a day, at times through cold rain and wind, and at one point amidst a great buffalo herd. Nevertheless, French's decision had been a good one—three days later, when they arrived at the west butte, they found plenty of water and grass. Sadly, for a number of the horses it was too late—so many died there that the men called the site "Dead Horse Coulee."

While the divisions were heading for the Sweet Grass Hills, French took Assistant Commissioner Macleod, two officers, guide Pierre Léveillé, plus four carts, and rode 145 kilometres south to Fort Benton, Montana, to buy supplies, purchase horses, use the telegraph services to contact Ottawa and hire another reliable guide. French decided that once he was done in Montana, he would return east with Troops D and E to arrange for winter headquarters and look into finding permanent western headquarters. He would direct Macleod to lead the remaining Troops B, C and F to deal with Fort Whoop-Up, after which they would stay and build their own fort in the area. French felt a continuing presence of the mounted police would stop the return of whisky traders.

At Fort Benton, a telegraph from the Canadian government was waiting for French, confirming his orders to march east to Swan River (near Fort Pelly), where he was told a "fine barracks" was being built for the NWMP headquarters. French returned to Canada the next day, September 25, and headed back east.

Macleod stayed at Fort Benton long enough to hire the legendary Jerry Potts, a short, bowlegged Métis who had an uncanny ability to lead as a guide and scout. Skilled in several Native languages, he became the Force's chief interpreter and for the next 22 years played a key role in communication and treaty negotiations with the prairie First Nations. Potts was no fan of the whisky traders, having worked at Fort Whoop-Up and seen first-hand the problems that whisky brought to Native people. In fact, his own father, mother and half-brother had all been murdered because of whisky.

Potts agreed to work for the NWMP for $90 a month because he believed the Mounties were serious about putting an end to whisky smuggling and bringing peace to the West, and he liked that. He promised to bring Macleod and the three divisions to Fort Whoop-Up. He then led the men in an 80-kilometre march, arriving on October 9 at a river bluff overlooking the 'real' Fort Whoop-Up. Upon their arrival, Macleod was ready to launch a massive assault with his men and field guns, but Potts suggested that they "just ride in."

It was a strangely quiet scene as the Mounties approached the fort. Concerned that this stillness might be a trap, Macleod prepared for battle. He positioned the field guns to aim at the fort and placed the troops in skirmish battle lines. Then, when Potts signalled Macleod, the two of them rode up to the huge timber doors. Macleod knocked and, to his surprise, the gate immediately opened. There to greet the two men was the fort's agent, Dave Akers, who invited them to come inside and then offered all the Mounties a hot meal and fresh vegetables.

Akers, a Dutch-American, was one of the original whisky traders in the country. He had run away to California when he was young and had made about $60,000 in gold dust. However, the story goes that as he was heading back to the eastern US to marry his girlfriend, his gold-dust bag was stolen. Broke, he headed back west.

Macleod ordered his men to search Fort Whoop-Up, but they found no liquor on site—it had all been removed in anticipation of the Mounties' arrival. And, except for Akers, the place was abandoned. Macleod liked the fort and offered to buy it from Akers for $10,000, intending to use it as the new police post. Akers made a counter-offer of $25,000, which Macleod refused.

With no agreement, the NWMP left the next morning to find a location on which to build their own fort. Potts led the men to an island on the Belly River (now the Oldman River); he said it was the best site for a new detachment. The men then began construction of the new fort, which they named Fort Macleod. It would be the first permanent Mountie post in Western Canada.

At the end of 1874, the Mounties had six posts in the West, with half of the Force members stationed at Fort Dufferin, Swan River, Fort Garry and Fort Ellice, and the remainder at Fort Edmonton (22 men) and Fort Macleod (150 men). In 1875, Fort Walsh was built a short distance upstream of the site of the Cypress Hills Massacre. It would serve as force headquarters from 1878 until 1882, with as many as 150 men serving in the garrison. In 1882, NWMP headquarters moved to Regina.

2

Prairie Policing

BY 1875, THE MOUNTIES HAD successfully destroyed most of the illegal whisky trade in Western Canada. Their focus now became administering law and order to the northwest, assisting new settlers homesteading in the area and fostering positive relationships with the Native peoples of the Prairies.

While it was important that the NWMP develop goodwill with Native leaders as a way to maintain security and peace on the Prairies, there was another, more political reason. Positive relations with the area's First Nations would make it easier to deliver the government's Native agenda—the signing of treaties in which the First Nations would cede land to the federal government.

Crowfoot and Red Crow

The early years of the NWMP set the tone for how law and order was to be delivered in the West. The mounted police-men had been posted on the stomping grounds of many of the proudest and most warlike First Nations in the West and were ordered by the Canadian government to establish friendly relations.

The man tasked with convincing the Native chiefs of the Force's good intentions was Assistant Commissioner James Macleod. Born on the Isle of Skye in Scotland, Macleod had immigrated to Upper Canada with his parents when he was 9 years old. He became a lawyer at the age of 26 and in 1873 joined the NWMP as one of the original nine commissioned officers. At that time, he had already had 18 years of militia experience, including service during the 1870 Red River Rebellion.

After meeting the physical demands of the March West and the search for Fort Whoop-Up, Macleod was now under a different kind of command pressure that demanded his best diplomatic skills: he had to gain the support of the Blackfoot Confederacy, comprised of the Blackfoot (Siksika), Blood (Kainaiwa), Peigan (Piikani), Sarcee (Tsuu T'ina) and Stoney (Bearpaw, Chiniki, Wesley, Goodstoney) tribes. It would be up to him to convince the chiefs that the NWMP had come in peace as their friends, not enemies.

If Native leaders like the powerful Chief Crowfoot of the

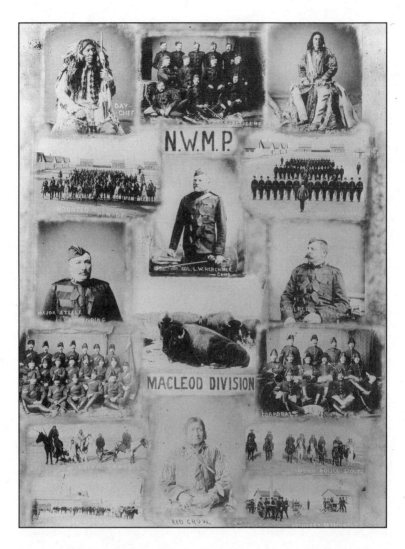

A composite image celebrating the achievements of the Macleod division of the NWMP. Major Sam Steele is pictured on the left.

Blackfoot or the influential Chief Red Crow of the Blood chose to oppose the NWMP, the Prairies would likely become a battleground with bloody confrontations between Canadian government forces and First Nations similar to what happened in the United States. Crowfoot and Red Crow's ability to recognize the tides of change—and their ability to see how their people could live and benefit from these changes—would be critical to any peaceful transition. Would they agree to negotiation, compromise, accommodation and peace, or would they choose to go to war? Macleod knew his relationship with them would play a pivotal role in their decision.

The Native peoples of the Prairies had first heard about the impending arrival of the mounted police from pioneer Methodist missionary Reverend John McDougall. He had been asked to inform them of the police's good intentions, and although the Native leaders had promised not to attack the Mounties, they said they would monitor them. So when the NWMP arrived at the Belly River on October 13, 1874, Assistant Commissioner McLeod knew that keen eyes were watching their every movement as they began constructing their stockaded fort. Soon, Native sentries were in plain view, sitting on their horses at the river's edge or on the hillside above, watching the Mounties toil. Macleod knew that his actions, and those of his men, were being discussed in Native councils and by their campfires.

The first chiefs who came to visit Macleod at the partially completed fort were from the Blood and Peigan tribes, sent perhaps by Crowfoot to spy and bring back information. Macleod met with them and through Jerry Potts explained that the Mounties had come to get rid of the whisky traders and bring peace to their country.

Then the powerful Red Crow visited Macleod and wanted to know how the NWMP would operate. When Macleod explained to him the Mounties' principle of justice for all, regardless of race, Red Crow pledged his cooperation.

But the chief that Macleod was hoping would soon visit was the shrewd Crowfoot, the dominant leader of the Blackfoot Confederacy. Renowned for his wisdom and bravery, Crowfoot's word was law throughout a territory that today stretches across southern Alberta.

Finally, on December 1, 1874, Crowfoot rode into Fort Macleod to visit *Stamix Otokan* or "Bull's Head," the name already given to Macleod by the Blackfoot (perhaps because of the bull's head mounted over the door to his quarters). Macleod knew in advance that the great chief was coming to visit and welcomed him with honour, having directed all his men to wear their scarlet dress uniforms. Crowfoot made it clear, however, that he was there as neither friend nor foe. Rather, he had come with an open mind to hear about these men riding horses and wearing scarlet uniforms—why they had come, what they were going to do and how long they would stay. It was agreed that a powwow would be held a few days later, at which time Macleod was expected to address these issues.

When Crowfoot returned for the powwow, he brought with him the mightiest of the Peigan and Blood chiefs. After formal introductions, handshakes and official greetings, they sat in a circle. Jerry Potts lit the peace pipe and passed it around, and then the serious dialogue began. The chiefs had come to hear Macleod talk. With Potts acting as his interpreter, Macleod said, "I come from the Great White Queen [Queen Victoria]. I come in friendship."

Macleod explained that the Mounties had come to the Prairies to stop whisky trading, to establish the Great White Queen's laws and to bring peace and order to the country. He told the chiefs that the NWMP would remain at Fort Macleod to enforce the Queen's laws and emphasized that they would punish anyone—white or Native—who refused to obey these laws. Macleod assured the chiefs that no Native people would receive punishment for breaking laws that they did not understand or for actions that they did not know to be wrong. He then told them that murder, horse stealing and war were wrong and that these crimes had to stop. "If one of your young men does wrong, we will arrest him, bring him to be tried by her laws. You may come to see he is fairly tried."

Finally, Macleod made it clear to the chiefs that the Mounties had not come to steal the Native peoples' land. If the government wanted any land, it would send men to discuss and make treaties with the First Nations.

The 44-year-old Crowfoot, with his penetrating eyes

and chiselled features, listened carefully as he tried to understand the concept of a police force. He asked straight, blunt questions, and Macleod gave him direct answers.

Then, after a long silence, Crowfoot responded to Macleod: "My brother, your words make me glad. I listened to them not only with my ears but with my heart also. In the coming of the Long Knives, with their firewater and quick-shooting guns, we are weak and our people have been woefully slain and impoverished. You say this will be stopped. We are glad to have it stopped. What you tell us about this strong power which will govern good law and treat the Indian same as the white man, makes us glad to hear. My brother, I believe you and I am thankful."

Treaty Negotiations

Chief Crowfoot's influence and power were most evident three years later, during the negotiations for Treaty Seven between the chiefs of the Blackfoot Confederacy and the Canadian government, represented by Lieutenant Governor David Laird and NWMP commissioner James Macleod.

On September 19, 1877, at Blackfoot Crossing on the Bow River, Crowfoot and the chiefs began negotiations with Laird and Macleod while 4,000 to 5,000 Native people gathered and waited. For the next few days, Macleod and Laird answered questions regarding details of the treaty and clarifying issues like ownership of the Native reserves, timber and coal rights and Native rights to hunt anywhere over the

Prairies. The government would offer reserves and assistance to Native peoples if the Natives would deed their land to the government.

On September 21, in the early afternoon, a hush fell over the crowd as Crowfoot rose to announce whether he would sign the treaty: "If the police had not come to this country, where would we all be now? Bad men and whisky were killing us so fast that very few of us would have been alive today. The Mounted Police have protected us as the feathers of the bird protect it from the frosts of winter. I wish all my people good and trust that all our hearts will increase in goodness from this time forward. I am satisfied. I am satisfied. I will sign the Treaty."

Next, Red Crow prepared to speak. He had been somewhat reluctant to sign, feeling the offer was less than ideal. He and Crowfoot had spent the previous night discussing the treaty, and now he was ready with his decision: "Three years ago when the Mounted Police came to my country, I met and shook hands with Stamix Otokan at the Belly River. Since then he has made me many promises and kept them all—not one of them has been broken. Everything that the Mounted Police have done has been for our good. I trust Stamix Otokan and will leave everything to him."

Because the two most influential of their leaders had accepted the treaty, the other chiefs also agreed to endorse it. The next day, September 22, Treaty Seven was officially signed.

Until his death on April 25, 1890, Crowfoot kept his word to stand by the NWMP. When American Sioux asked Crowfoot to join in violence against Canadian white people, he declined. And when Louis Riel tried to solicit support from Crowfoot for the 1885 North-West Rebellion, Crowfoot declined once again.

Red Crow also continued to follow the path of peace. "We have had enough war. I think we can live without it. If civilization can tame the buffalo so that they are like cattle, the lesson is one that I should not forget."

Crowfoot and Red Crow were both intelligent, visionary leaders. If the NWMP had not been able to gain their friendship and support, it would have been difficult—perhaps impossible—for the Mounties to bring change to Western Canada without violence.

The American Sioux Arrive

While relations between the NWMP and the prairie Native peoples got off to a positive start, the amicable atmosphere was soon threatened when the American Sioux—traditional enemies of many Canadian First Nations—decided to come to Canada.

In the United States, the relationships between Native peoples, white settlers and the government were often confrontational and violent. For years, the American Sioux had been fighting to stop white settlers from taking their traditional lands. In 1875, they were ordered to leave their homelands and relocate to reserve land or else be labelled enemies of the United States. When the Sioux refused to leave, the United States Army stepped in to physically move them.

In June 1876, the situation became deadly with the Battle of Little Big Horn, fought between the Sioux and five companies of the 7th US Cavalry under the command of Lieutenant Colonel George A. Custer. On June 25, led by the legendary Chief Sitting Bull, the Sioux trapped and killed all 265 soldiers and civilians under Custer's command. The Canadian government feared the American Sioux would seek refuge in Canada after the Battle of Little Big Horn. And if this did indeed turn out to be the case, the Mounties were expected to deal with them.

How the NWMP managed the arrival of the American Sioux and its feared Chief Sitting Bull became one of the defining moments in Mountie history. The key players were Inspector James Walsh, in command of both Fort Walsh and the nearby Wood Mountain detachment, and Chief Sitting Bull, the most feared and powerful chief in North America.

The NWMP were ready for the influx of American Sioux. Reinforcements were in place, the post was fortified and scouts monitored the border closely. In late November 1876, when news reached Fort Walsh that a large party of Sioux was moving north towards Wood Mountain, Walsh and 15 Mounties rode eight days from Fort Walsh to get to the site. By the time they got there in early December, about 3,000 Sioux, along with 3,500 horses and 30 US government mules, were camped close to the nearby trading post.

Walsh and his men rode right into the camp and asked to speak to the tribe's hereditary chief, Black Moon. The Sioux called a council and explained to Walsh how they were tired of being hunted; they had come to the land of the Great White Mother to find refuge. Walsh then laid out the conditions they would have to meet in order to stay in Canada: obey Canadian laws, keep peace with Canadian Native tribes, and, in particular, do not use Canada as a base to attack the United States.

For the rest of the winter, the NWMP patrolled and monitored the area as they waited for Sitting Bull to arrive.

Walsh and Sitting Bull

In May 1877, the NWMP received word that Sitting Bull had settled 95 kilometres southeast of Fort Walsh. Inspector Walsh immediately rode out to meet him, taking along Sergeant Robert McCutcheon, three constables and two scouts.

On May 7, three days later after leaving the fort, Walsh and his men were following Sitting Bull's trail, which led from the Montana border to the hills and ravines of Pinto Horse Butte. Around noon that day, they realized they were being watched by mounted Sioux, who were sitting motionless on the hilltops. As the small group rode on, more Sioux appeared on the hills until Walsh and his men were completely surrounded. None of the Sioux, however, made any attempts to stop the NWMP.

Walsh and his men kept going until they rounded a hill and came upon the edge of a Native camp. Calmly, they reined in and sat mounted while a group of Sioux riders approached them. Spotted Eagle, one of the chiefs, told them they were the first white men to ride into Sitting Bull's camp. Walsh asked to meet Sitting Bull, and a short while later the famous chief arrived. He looked to be in his 40s, with a muscular build on a 5-foot 10-inch frame; he was bowlegged and walked with a limp. His eyes were alert, his nose prominent, his features well-defined and two braids of black hair hung down his shoulders. Greeting his visitors, he shook hands first with McCutcheon and then with Walsh.

The Mounties and the Sioux talked the rest of the day. When Sitting Bull was asked why he had come to Canada, he said to find peace and sanctuary in the White Mother's land. He reminded Walsh that after the War of 1812, the *Shagonosh*, or "British," Father (King George III) had told the Sioux they could move northward when they no longer wanted to live under the Americans. Sitting Bull's grandfather had fought alongside the British soldiers and had been told, "If you should ever wish to find peace, go north to the land of redcoats." Sitting Bull explained that he now considered himself and his people British subjects. But Walsh told him it was unlikely he could move to Canada permanently. Rather, the Sioux would someday have to return to the United States.

Walsh explained Canadian laws to Sitting Bull, as he had to Black Moon and the Sioux who had arrived earlier. He made it clear that Canadian laws had to be obeyed by everyone, regardless of race. He also insisted that the Sioux not make war with other tribes and that they refrain from stealing anything (including horses), from killing or injuring anyone and from using Canadian soil as a base to attack Americans. Sitting Bull liked what Walsh told him about the White Mother's laws, especially the principle of justice for all.

Walsh and his men stayed the night in Sitting Bull's camp. All seemed to go well until the next morning. The small group was about to ride back to their detachment when Solomon, one of the Métis police scouts, noticed five horses, probably all stolen, being brought into the Sioux camp by a trio of American Assiniboine (a branch of the Sioux). He recognized the leader of the trio as White Dog, who was considered such a great warrior that Sitting Bull had once offered him 300 horses to join his camp for the summer. Solomon and the other police scout, Léveillé, identified three of the horses as belonging to Father DeCorty, a Roman Catholic priest in Cypress Hills.

Once Solomon was convinced the horses were stolen, Walsh instructed McCutcheon to arrest the rustling trio.

Taking a few Mounties with him, McCutcheon walked over to White Dog, who was now standing with a group of 50 to 60 warriors. When McCutcheon tried to make the arrest, White Dog refused to cooperate. Sensing a difficult situation developing, Walsh joined McCutcheon, as did hundreds of Sioux who were curious to see what would happen next.

Walsh addressed White Dog sternly. "You say you will neither be arrested nor surrender these horses? I arrest you for theft."

With Sioux warriors gathered around him, White Dog was confident that the Mounties wouldn't dare take him away. But he underestimated Walsh's determination to uphold the law.

"Tell me where you got those horses, how you got them, and what you intend doing with them, or I'll clap these irons on you and take you away," said Walsh as he dangled leg irons in front of White Dog.

A hush fell over the camp. White Dog had expected the Sioux to rescue him, and his courage faltered when they didn't. He said that the horses had been wandering loose when he'd found them and that in America it was customary for the finder to keep a loose horse unless someone claimed it. His defence was that he didn't know he had done anything wrong.

Although Walsh did not believe him, he released White Dog, giving him the benefit of the doubt. The tense situation seemed resolved, but as White Dog turned to walk away, he muttered menacingly to the inspector in Sioux, "I shall meet you again."

Enraged, Walsh stopped White Dog and ordered him to repeat his words to the interpreter. White Dog refused, standing defiantly silent. Walsh asked him again, and again White Dog kept quiet. Then, lifting the leg irons high, Walsh said, "White Dog, withdraw those words, or I shall put you in irons and take you to Fort Walsh for threatening a police officer."

Begrudgingly, White Dog apologized, saying his words were not meant to be a threat. Walsh knew he was lying, but accepted the apology. He felt that by making an example of White Dog and by not backing down or showing any fear, he had sent a clear message to the Sioux: Canadian law would be enforced. As a result, Sitting Bull and the Sioux admired his determination.

Sitting Bull did not leave Canada and surrender to American military authorities until July 18, 1881. Three years later, he took up residence along the Grand River, in present-day South Dakota, where he was killed by tribal police on December 15, 1890. Despite their differences, Walsh and Sitting Bull had a strong friendship. After Sitting Bull's death, Walsh wrote, "Bull had been misrepresented. He was not the bloodthirsty man reports made him out to be. He asked for nothing but justice. He was not a cruel man. He was kind of heart. He was not dishonest. He was truthful. He loved his people and was glad to give his hand in friendship to any man who was honest with him."

Handling Trouble

Within days of returning to Fort Walsh after his historic meeting with Sitting Bull, Inspector Walsh again rode out to meet American Natives. But this time, it was to stop violence being committed against Canadian Native peoples.

The problem centred on a group of American Assiniboine who had crossed into Canada to hunt buffalo. This group had set their 250 lodges beside the 15 lodges of a Saulteaux camp located at the northwest end of Wood Mountain. An Assiniboine warrior named Crow's Dance threatened and demanded obedience from Saulteaux chief Little Child. The Saulteaux leader refused, replying that he only obeyed the laws of the "White Chief of Fort Walsh." He then ordered his people to start breaking up their camp so that they could move away from the Assiniboine.

The angry Assiniboine decided to show muscle. They attacked the Saulteaux, firing guns, killing 19 sled dogs, slashing tepees and knocking down anyone who got in the way. Crow's Dance then warned the Saulteaux, "And if the redcoats come, we'll cut out the White Chief's heart and eat it."

The tough talk didn't scare Little Child. He rode 80 kilometres to report the incident to the NWMP. Walsh responded by riding back with Little Child, accompanied by 15 NWMP members and scout Louis Léveillé. They halted when they could see the Assiniboine encampment about two kilometres away, in a valley below. Crow's Dance's war lodge was in the middle of the camp.

Walsh ordered pistols and carbines loaded. Strategically, he positioned some of his men on a small butte about one kilometre from the camp. Then, silently in the night, Walsh and the rest of the men rode down a ravine towards the camp. As they got closer, the inspector signalled the group to "sharp trot," and they quickly surrounded the war lodge. Before any of the sleeping warriors could react, Walsh and his men seized Crow's Dance, another chief by the name of Crooked Arm and the men with them and carried them to the nearby butte where the other NWMP members were waiting. The prisoners were handcuffed and the butte position was fortified with rocks and earth.

It was only 5 a.m. The NWMP had been so lightning-quick in their actions that the rest of the Assiniboine in the camp continued to sleep, unaware that anything out of the ordinary had taken place.

Instead of returning to Fort Walsh with his prisoners, Inspector Walsh waited awhile and then sent Léveillé back to the camp to ask the other Assiniboine chiefs to come to the butte for a meeting. When they did, they brought along an angry crowd of Assiniboine. Walsh told them that under the White Mother's laws, every person had the freedom of movement in this country. Then, after demanding that the Assiniboine never again force their will on the Saulteaux, he informed the angry crowd that the NWMP would be taking Crow's Dance and 12 others as prisoners for trial at Fort Walsh. As Walsh and his men rode away, the Assinibone did not interfere.

Later, Walsh released 11 of the warriors with a warning, while Crow's Dance and Chief Crooked Arm received short prison terms.

The Deadly Power of the Windigo

As they strove to bring peace and justice to the Prairies, the Mounties not only had to prevent entire tribes from warring against each other, they also had to ensure that individuals who broke the law were brought to justice. In 1879, one such individual was sent to the gallows at the NWMP detachment at Fort Saskatchewan.

In March of that year, a tall, muscular Cree by the name of Swift Runner arrived at the Roman Catholic mission at St. Albert and reported that nine members of his family, including his wife and six children, had all died of starvation that winter. The priests knew that the past winter had been brutally cold, and with no buffalo herds to hunt, many Native people were starving. But they were nevertheless suspicious of Swift Runner—he looked surprisingly healthy, despite the fact that he claimed to have survived by chewing rawhide and drinking broth that he'd made by boiling his tepee.

The priests allowed Swift Runner to stay at the mission, and Reverend Father Hippolyte Leduc listened to the Cree man as he told of nightmares in which the evil spirit of the Windigo was trying to possess him. It wasn't until Swift Runner asked for permission to take the children of the mission on a traditional hunting trip that the priests became alarmed. They asked the NWMP at Fort Saskatchewan to find out how Swift Runner's family members had actually died.

In Native mythology, the Windigo is an evil spirit that possesses a person and causes him or her to hunger for human flesh. Many Native peoples believed that if a human body became possessed by the Windigo, it had to be burned to ashes in order to stop the evil spirit's hunger. Once the evil spirit tasted human flesh, it only craved more.

The priests no longer believed Swift Runner's story about his family dying of starvation, and neither did Inspector William D. Jarvis. On May 27, Jarvis arrested the Cree man for murder and brought him to Fort Saskatchewan for questioning. Swift Runner stuck with the same starvation story, so the NWMP organized a search party to gather evidence at his winter camp near the Sturgeon River.

Led by Sub-Inspector Severe Gagnon and Sergeant Richard Steele (the younger brother of Sam Steele), the group left Fort Saskatchewan on June 4, with Swift Runner shackled inside a Red River cart. Twice he tried to escape, and twice he was recaptured. He continued to insist that his family had died of starvation, but when they arrived in the area of the camp, Swift Runner led them in circles during the search.

Finally, the Métis interpreter made a drink concoction of plug tobacco soaked in strong tea and told Sub-Inspector Gagnon to give it to the prisoner, explaining that the "medicine" would make Swift Runner tell them everything. The interpreter was right. After taking the drink, Swift Runner "threw back his head, howled like a wolf and led the police to a camp in the bush"—a ghastly death camp where human skulls and bones were scattered around the campfire ashes and a nearby cooking pot was coated with human fat. Horrified, the Mounties realized that Swift Runner had slaughtered and eaten his entire family.

Swift Runner was charged with murder. At his trial on August 16, the evidence against him was so overwhelming that the six-man jury convicted him after only a half hour of deliberations. He was sentenced to die on December 20.

In his final weeks, as Father Leduc was ministering to him, Swift Runner confessed to the murders, but sincerely felt it had been the spirit of the Windigo that had committed the atrocious crimes. He told of how he had first killed and eaten one of his sons, then his wife and four children, his brother and mother. Initially he had spared his 7-year-old son, who had joined him in eating the others. In the spring, however, as father and son were approaching Egg Lake, near today's Morinville, Swift Runner panicked that someone would find out what he had done, so he shot and ate his last remaining son. He explained to Father Leduc, "The devil took possession of my soul and I saw my son as a fat beaver."

While he was in custody, Swift Runner's behaviour swung from unpredictable and erratic to jovial. At times he joked about his crime, telling the guard "what fine eating he would make." He seemed particularly attracted to 21-year-old Constable Fred Bagley, the only one who could speak Cree. The night before his execution, Swift Runner presented Bagley with his beaded and furred war club and his smoking pipe.

It was -42°C when Swift Runner was hanged on the morning of December 20. Bagley later described the Cree's last hour: "His surviving relatives and a number of specially invited chiefs sat in a circle within the fort furiously drumming and singing the death song to speed their departing brother on his way to the happy hunting grounds. As he stood on the scaffold, the murderer expressed his thanks to the Mounted Police and the priests (who had received him into the Roman Catholic Church after the trial) for their kindness to him and urged his own people to take warning from his fate."

Swift Runner was the first person to be executed by the NWMP.

The First Murder

Mountie history recorded another tragic first in 1879—the first murder of a Mountie, young Constable Marmaduke Graburn. Constable Graburn was 18 years old when he joined the NWMP in Ottawa with his friend Gordon Johnson. They were both sworn in at Fort Walsh on June 9,

1879, and Graburn was posted for duty at the fort's main horse camp, where the NWMP horses were kept for rehabilitation and rest.

On the afternoon of November 17, 1879, it seemed that Graburn had a verbal disagreement with a Blood man called Star Child who was begging for food at the horse camp. Graburn ordered the man to leave. Sometime later, the detachment was alarmed to see the young constable's horse return saddled and bridled, but with no rider.

A search party led by Jerry Potts followed a bloody trail that led to the discovery of Graburn's body. He had been shot twice at close range through the back of the head. Unfortunately, a chinook wind had swept through the area, melting some of the snow and destroying any further tracks. The murder investigation ground to a halt before it had even begun.

Six months later, two Bloods were arrested for stealing horses and placed in jail at Fort Walsh. No one had been charged yet with Graburn's murder, and both men were afraid that the frustrated Mounties would charge them with the crime. In order to prevent this possibility, they decided to tell the police the name of the murderer. It was midnight when they asked to meet with Superintendent Crozier to tell him all they knew about the killing. Before they would talk, however, the frightened men asked police to cover the windows—someone from the Blood Nation, or maybe even the murderer, might be lurking outside.

The two prisoners told Crozier that the murderer was Star Child, and that he had fled across the border for refuge in the Bear Paw Mountains. The Mounties asked the United States authorities to arrest Star Child, but the sheriff demanded $5,000 first and was declined. Star Child remained at large, safe across the American border.

A year later, when he returned to Canada and joined the Blood Nation near Fort Macleod, four Mounties (including Corporal Patterson) and Jerry Potts launched a surprise attack at dawn to arrest him. They entered his lodge stealthily, but before they could handcuff him, he discharged a rifle shot to warn the other warriors. Quickly, Patterson picked Star Child up and carried him out to his horse. As the Mounties and Potts rode out of the camp, the Blood warriors were right behind them in hot pursuit. At full gallop for 40 kilometres, the police raced to Fort Macleod, trying desperately to keep ahead of the warriors. It was a hard, exhausting ride, but their lives were at risk so they had to win the race to the fort's gate—and they did.

At his trial, the evidence against Star Child was strong, and he even confessed to the murder. Nevertheless, the six-man jury of ranchers and settlers—fearful of revenge by the Blood—found him not guilty. The official report on the first murder of a Mountie to die a violent death while on duty reads, "Murdered by person or persons unknown ..."

Not long after his first trial, Star Child was convicted of horse stealing and sentenced to 14 years in Stony Mountain

Penitentiary. Following his release, the NWMP hired him as a scout.

Constable Graburn is buried at Fort Walsh (now a National Historic Site) and a cairn in Cypress Hills Park marks where he died. At the Beechwood Cemetery in Ottawa, the inscription on his memorial stone reads "Marmaduke Graburn – Primus Moriri (First to die)."

CHAPTER

3

Policing the Klondike

BEFORE THE 1890S, THE YUKON was unofficially controlled by a kind of frontier justice administered during local miners' meetings. These were a basic form of self-government, where everyone had one vote and decisions were made by majority vote. The first Yukon miners' meeting was held around 1886 at the Stewart River Trading Post, operated by traders Leroy McQuesten and Arthur Harper. However, when whisky traders began to appear in the area in the 1890s, the miners moved their meetings to saloons, where they could drink while voting.

The federal government, concerned about sovereignty and missed revenue from customs duties, sent Inspector Charles Constantine to the Yukon in 1894 to report on the conditions there. An excellent choice for the task, Constantine had been part of the 1870 Red River Expedition (alongside Sam Steele, James Macleod and James Walsh) and was appointed Manitoba's first chief of police that same year. Constantine joined the NWMP in 1885, after having served in a volunteer military regiment during the 1885 North-West Rebellion.

Constantine reported that the Yukon could be controlled if at least 50 specially selected men were assigned to set up a northern detachment. He recommended a detachment of two officers, six non-commissioned officers (NCOs), a surgeon and 35 to 40 men. The government complied with this request—at least partly. The following summer, Constantine was ordered to return to the Yukon with 19 men.

In July of 1895, Inspector Constantine, his wife and the NWMP group (comprised of Inspector D.A.E. Strickland, Assistant Surgeon A.E. Wells and 17 non-commissioned officers and men) sailed an ocean steamer up the Pacific Coast to the mouth of the Yukon River in Alaska and then took another steamer upstream for a further 2,400 kilometres. Once they arrived near Dawson City, they started construction of their new detachment, cutting logs 90 kilometres upstream and then floating them down the Yukon River. By November, nine buildings were finished, but none were too comfortable. Inside, winter temperatures averaged zero degrees and the mud roofs leaked dirty water whenever there was a thaw. The new police post was called Fort Constantine,

Superintendent Charles Constantine, back row, fourth from left, at Fort Constantine, Yukon Territory, ca. 1890s.

and at the time it was the most northerly police post in the British Empire.

Constantine quickly got to work, taking on multiple roles he called "Chief Magistrate, Commander-in-Chief, and Home and Foreign Secretary." Besides investigating crimes, the small detachment was kept busy collecting customs duties, gold royalties and miners' fees. The men also spent time looking for smuggled liquor, acting as coroners and delivering mail.

In 1896, a year after the Mounties' arrival, the world's most famous gold stampede, the Klondike Gold Rush, was set in motion when a placer miner named George Carmack and his party, including Tagish Charley and Skookum Jim, discovered gold on Rabbit Creek (renamed Bonanza Creek), a small tributary off the Klondike River. Thanks to the pioneering police work of Constantine and his 19 men, law and order was already established in the Yukon; the NWMP were ready for the gold seekers.

During the winters of 1897 and 1898, tens of thousands of prospectors arrived from around the world to seek their fortune on the Klondike goldfields. Most came up the Pacific Coast and began their trek on American soil, travelling 30 kilometres up the Coastal Mountains by following either the Chilkoot or White Pass routes to the summit boundary on the Alaska–British Columbia border. There they crossed into Canada, where it was downhill for another 40 kilometres or more to Lake Bennett and the frozen headwaters of the Yukon River. Suffering through winter temperatures that averaged –40°C, and icy north winds that made the air even colder, they camped at these headwaters until spring. While they waited for the weather to warm, everyone in the area kept busy by building boats to travel downstream to the Klondike as soon as the ice broke.

The staggering number of people streaming into the Yukon prompted Inspector Constantine to request more men, and he got them. At the end of 1897, there were 8 officers and 88 men serving in the Yukon; a year later, the strength had increased to 10 officers and 254 men. To effectively police their huge jurisdiction, the NWMP went on to establish a chain of posts from Chilkoot all the way to Dawson City.

Building a Road to Nowhere

In 1897, Inspector Constantine recommended that an investigation be launched into developing an inland, all-Canadian route from Edmonton to the Yukon. Such a route would give Canadians an alternative way to the goldfields—a backdoor entry to the Klondike—without having to travel on American soil or trek over the dangerous Chilkoot or White Pass routes. Edmonton residents, anxious to cash in on the gold rush, were also pressuring the federal government to build such a route. Some gold seekers were already attempting to forge a 2,000-kilometre trail that started in Edmonton, but with no mapped or clear route to guide them, many became lost, some died, and others simply gave up.

While Constantine was doing his best to maintain law and order among the thousands of gold seekers, the Canadian government acted on his recommendation and directed the NWMP to undertake a survey patrol from Edmonton via the Peace River to the Yukon and to report back on the route's feasibility.

The commissioner at the time was 57-year-old Lawrence William Herschmer, a British-born United Empire Loyalist who had been appointed to the Mounties' top post on April 1, 1886. Herschmer instructed 55-year-old Inspector

J.D. Moodie to lead the difficult expedition. Moodie chose his patrol carefully, as these men would need extraordinary endurance and stamina to complete the long trek into unknown wilderness. He selected Constable Frank J. Fitzgerald; Special Constables Richard Hardisty, Frank Lafferty and H.S. Tobin; and Baptiste Pepin, a Métis hired to manage the pack train of 31 horses.

The expedition's list of objectives was daunting, reading more like a job list for an experienced survey and road-building crew rather than a group of policemen. It included developing a map showing the best route from Edmonton to the headwaters of the Pelly River, including the best trail for wagons as well as good grazing sites and hunting areas; identifying areas requiring further grading, ditching and bridge-building; and compiling a solid "everything-you-need-to-know" information package for future travellers of the route.

Commissioner Herschmer laid out the wilderness-breaking route they would follow: Edmonton to Peace River to Fort St. John, across the Rockies to Finlay River, north along Finlay River to Fort Grahame, and then over Sifton Pass to Sylvester Landing on the Dease River. Once they reached the Dease River, it would be up to Moodie to choose the final route to the Pelly River. There was no room for failure in the expedition, and Herschmer's order to Moodie was simple: just get there.

Moodie and his men left Edmonton on September 8,

1897, on what would become a 14-month test of physical endurance. Battling bitterly cold temperatures and the elements of weather, they chopped their way through fallen timber, slashed through brush, searched the woods for wandering packhorses, made bridges, crossed raging rivers and trekked through thick muskeg. Author Dick North wrote in *The Lost Patrol* that Moodie's party "took on the semblance of a mini-construction company, where the functions of one hundred men were combined in only six, without the benefit of mechanization."

When the small group of Mounties reached the fast-moving Peace River, they built a raft to cross, but the current swept the raft 450 metres downstream, forcing the men to laboriously pull it back upstream by hand. Even after they retrieved the raft their troubles weren't over. Next they had to swim the horses across the cold, swift waters, but only 10 of the 31 horses would cross. The others balked, refusing to enter the river. After many attempts to get them across, the men had no choice but to leave them on the other side and seek help at nearby Fort St. John. Later, the Mounties returned to the horses with an HBC flat-bottomed riverboat and, using ropes, led them across the river.

After buying an additional 33 dogs and 5 sleighs, the patrol left Fort St. John on December 2, heading up the Peace River to the Halfway River, then up the Halfway to Frances Lake. Fort Grahame was still over 640 kilometres away. On Christmas Day they reached the headwaters of the Halfway

River, and by the end of December they were forced to start butchering their horses in order to feed the dogs.

It was a brutal journey. The men had to constantly break trail through deep snow. When they came across lengthy canyons with impassable rapids, they had to make long detours, adding to their exhaustion. They got lost at one point and travelled 45 kilometres unnecessarily, while temperatures hovered between –34 and –40°C. Sickness and accidents plagued them. On four occasions, Moodie suffered from bouts of snow blindness.

They ran out of food for themselves and the dogs on January 17, but the next day, fortunately, they finally reached Fort Grahame. However, the news that greeted them there was not good—the HBC clerk, William Fox, had plenty of food for the men, but none for the dogs. Fox suggested the Mounties go ice fishing for the dog food, so Constable Fitzgerald took the dogs to a lake 30 kilometres southwest of Fort Grahame and, for the next month, fished for their food. He returned to the fort on February 11.

The food situation was still so desperate that Moodie decided to go south and replenish their supplies. Taking four of his men with him, he left for Stuart Lake on April 1, leaving only Fitzgerald at Fort Grahame. During the trip, Moodie came down with such severe snow blindness that his eyes had to remain bandaged for four days, and he had to be pulled on a sleigh.

On July 7, 1898, more than two months after leaving

Fort Grahame, the five men returned with a replenished food supply. Eight days later, the patrol continued towards the Pelly River using hired packhorses, having killed all their own horses to feed the dogs. But it would be October 1—four months later—before they finally reached their destination.

By this time, they had been on the patrol for 13 months, and they still weren't finished. Now they would have to travel downstream to Fort Selkirk. (Back at NWMP headquarters, there was a fear that the men had perished, as there had been no communication with the expedition.)

The haggard, weather-beaten party returned the horses to the Native owners, cached their packsaddles and other surplus goods and started paddling their canvas canoe down the Pelly River. But trouble continued to plague them. The rapids and floating ice punctured the canoe until it was wrecked. Moodie then transferred two men and some supplies to a small raft, but the raft capsized. They built a bigger raft, but that became blocked in the ice channels. Finally, they had a stroke of luck when a group of prospectors chanced by and Moodie was able to purchase their Peterborough canoe for $450. Still, valuable time had already been lost on canoe repairs and portaging over ice-glazed boulders.

When the river started to freeze and the strong downstream current took them to the edge of a 10-kilometre-long ice jam, almost sucking them underneath, Moodie ordered the men off the water. They were exhausted, hungry and

Canadian customs house at the summit of Chilkoot Pass, Alaska. Note the piles of supplies—the North-West Mounted Police would not allow prospectors into the Yukon Territory without enough food and supplies to last the winter.

cold, but it was still another 65 kilometres to Fort Selkirk. Desperate to finish their trek, they abandoned everything and, carrying only their "pack, ground-hog robe and extract of fluid beef," started to walk the remaining distance. As experienced northern travellers, they knew not to panic, but rather to conserve their strength by plodding slowly through the deep snow.

Two days and nights later, the exhausted patrol reached Fort Selkirk on October 24—14 months and 2,500 kilometres after they had left Edmonton. Soon after they arrived at Selkirk, Moodie spotted Colonel Evans of the Yukon Expeditionary Force. He walked up to the colonel and said, "How are you Evans?"

"Who are you?" Evans replied with surprise. When Moodie identified himself, Evans exclaimed, "Oh! Good God, you are all dead six months ago."

Not surprisingly, Moodie later reported the following regarding the all-Canadian route: "I should say the overland route would never be used in the face of the quick and easy one via Skagway."

The government stopped further development of the treacherous overland route to the Klondike, and the trail established by Moodie's patrol was forgotten—until later.

Ton of Goods

In 1897, as Moodie and his men were just beginning their overland adventure, ex-inspector James M. Walsh arrived in the Klondike to serve as the territory's first commissioner. By that time, Walsh had been gone from policing for 15 years and had been working as a coal dealer in Winnipeg. Now, as commissioner, he was responsible for the NMWP in the Yukon.

Arriving in the area in early winter, Walsh headed to Dawson City to start his new duties, but, much to his dismay, he was prevented from reaching his post on time—river ice forced his government party to overwinter near Big Salmon with few supplies. The experience led Walsh to order the police to turn back anyone at the mountain passes who did not have a year's supply of food and equipment with them. This rule became known as the famous "ton of goods" criteria (three pounds per day per person, plus equipment and tools) that had to be met by everyone crossing into Canada.

Early in 1898, the NWMP set up detachments at the summits of Chilkoot Pass and White Pass, right at the international boundary. The Union Jack was hoisted on February 25, 1898, at the Chilkoot Pass post and two days later at the White Pass post. There was no mistaking the NWMP presence at these two frontier posts, the points of entry onto Canadian soil. The police were there to collect customs duty and ensure that each person had a "ton of goods" and knew they had to obey Canadian laws.

Sam Steele, Lion of the North

February 1898 was a notable month for the NWMP in the Klondike for reasons beyond the building of detachments and the hoisting of Union Jacks. It was also during this month that the "Lion of the North," Sam Steele, arrived in the area.

Steele was already a legend by the time he arrived in the Yukon. Born in Upper Canada in 1849, he was known as one of the "original" Mounties, having joined the NWMP at its inception in 1873. Now at age 49, with 25 years of service, he had been involved in almost every significant event in the Canadian West, including the training of the first NWMP members, the March West of 1874, the North-West Rebellion of 1885 and the building of the CPR through the Rockies. Tall, barrel-chested, handsome and courageous, he personified the heroic image of the Mountie. A man of decisive action, he was a strong leader who was both respected and feared.

Superintendent Steele had been serving in southern Alberta when he received his orders in January 1898 to go north to the gold rush–crazy Yukon and, with Superintendent Aylesworth Bowen Perry, establish and then take command of the customs posts at Bennett Lake and the two Klondike passes.

Both the Chilkoot and White Passes were brutal mountain routes, but the rush of gold seekers kept growing nevertheless. In late March of 1898, Steele climbed the summit of White Pass and went down the Canadian side to Lake Bennett, where the two summit trails came together. He found over 10,000 people camped on both sides of the lake building boats, waiting for the Yukon River to thaw and for navigation to open.

With such a huge crowd of people gearing up to go down the Yukon River at the same time after ice break-up, Steele predicted absolute havoc—unless the NWMP developed a system to record and know the details about each boat. He ordered that every boat, canoe and scow in the region have a boat number painted clearly on the craft before it was launched. The NWMP would record each number in a register, along with the names of every man, woman and child onboard and the names and addresses of next of kin. The police would then check their lists at downstream posts. Failure to register a boat would be a major offence.

When the lake became clear of ice on May 29, the exodus of gold seekers downriver was an incredible scene. Steele watched from a hill behind the police post and counted "over 800 boats under sail on the 11½ miles of Lake Bennett." Later he wrote, "Strange and motley were these craft; large scows with oxen, cows, horses and dogs on board, well-built skiffs, clumsy, oblong tubs, little better than ordinary boxes; light and serviceable Peterboro' canoes ..."

But Steele knew the most dangerous part of the river journey was yet to come. The next day, he boarded the small steamer *Kilbourne* and took the river route to Miles Canyon (named in 1883 after Brigadier General Nelson A. Miles by American explorer Frederick Schwatka, who thought he was travelling in Alaska). Steele described the canyon as "a deep and dangerous gorge with perpendicular cliffs of granite, which no one could climb, and a current which ran like a mill race. The water, being closely confined, worked up into a ridge in the centre, which made the passage by small craft doubly dangerous." Just beyond the canyon were the treacherous White Horse Rapids (*Kwanlin* in Southern Tutchone), named by the Native people for the "flaxen hair and great strength" of a Finnish man who had drowned there.

When Steele arrived at Miles Canyon, he was greeted by a chaotic scene: several thousand boats were tied up in a jam at the mouth of the canyon, just past Canyon City, a small community with a police post, a roadhouse and a tramway office. Some prospectors had dared to run the canyon and rapids rather than portage or use the eight-kilometre tramline built in 1898. It followed the route of a First Nations portage that bypassed the canyon and river.

Most of the boat crews without whitewater experience had foolishly rushed to be first through the rapids, with deadly results: 150 boats had been smashed to pieces on the rocks and 10 men had drowned. Corporal Dixon and the Mounties at the Canyon City detachment had risked their lives to rescue men, women and children from the cold, fast-moving waters. Sadly, they could not save everyone.

To prevent more tragedy, Steele quickly developed an action plan. He gathered together the thousands of people (mostly Americans) who had tied up their boats, fearful of travelling any further. He then announced, "There are many of your countrymen who say that the Mounted Police make the laws as they go along, and I am going to do so now for your own good, therefore the directions that I give you shall be carried out strictly, and they are these ..."

He told the crowd that Corporal Dixon from the Canyon City detachment would immediately be in charge of passage on Miles Canyon and the White Horse Rapids. No woman or child would be allowed in any boat or canoe; instead, under police protection, they would have to walk the eight kilometres of grassy bank to the foot of the rapids. Corporal Dixon would also have to inspect and approve all loads before a boat could take passage. And no boat would be allowed to proceed without a registered river pilot selected by the NWMP (the pilots would be listed and serve on a rotation for a five-dollar fee).

The crowd liked what they heard. They got back into their boats and obeyed Steele's orders. It was due to the action of the NWMP at the Canyon City detachment and Steele's quick thinking that no more lives were lost or boats wrecked in Miles Canyon. By July of 1898, the venerable Steele had assumed command of all NWMP operations in the Yukon.

Bringing Out the Gold

By the end of the Klondike Gold Rush in 1898, the NWMP had processed over 30,000 people on the pass summits, inspected and checked over 30 million pounds of food and collected customs duties in excess of $150,000 in gold and notes.

Though the gold and cash collected was welcome income for the government, it nevertheless presented a problem to the NWMP. How could Force members manage to travel successfully through the crime-infested Alaskan towns of

Dyea and Skagway, past the gangster Soapy Smith and his men, in order to get the $150,000 safely to Victoria?

Sam Steele chose Inspector Zachary Taylor Wood to carry out the clandestine delivery mission on a route that would take him over the Chilkoot summit to Dyea and then by boat to Skagway, where a steamer would be waiting to take him to Victoria. (Wood was the great-grandson of the 12th president of the United States, and his son, Stuart Taylor Wood, would later become the 8th commissioner of the Force.)

The NWMP would escort Wood and his small group of men up to the Chilkoot summit, but from there the group was on its own. Wood adopted a low-profile approach, packing the gold and money in ordinary Mountie kit bags, which were so heavy it took a couple of men to carry each one. To provide a cover story and perhaps thwart a robbery attempt by Soapy's gang, the police spread a rumour that Wood was being transferred back to the Prairies and was taking his baggage and "boatmen" with him.

Jefferson "Soapy" Smith was a notorious criminal who ruled Skagway like a dictator. He had his own armed and disciplined army, a spy service and secret police. Soapy ran crooked gambling halls and bogus businesses (like linkless telegraph offices and freight companies that didn't haul anything) and never missed an opportunity to rob or fleece someone, often resorting to violence to get his way. Inspector Wood knew that Soapy would be more than willing to kill just about anyone to get his hands on the $150,000 in gold and notes.

Wood and his men left Dawson City on June 9, 1898. All went according to plan until they reached Dyea and hired a small boat to cross the bay to Skagway. From Skagway, they were to take the Canadian Pacific Railway steamer *Tartar* to Victoria. However, during the crossing from Dyea, a boatload of Soapy's thugs tried to run the men down and didn't back off until Wood threatened to shoot them.

There was more trouble waiting for Wood on the Skagway wharf. Soapy and more of his gunmen were on the dock, gathered midway between the *Tartar* and the spot where the Mounties had to land. Wood glanced over at the *Tartar* and was relieved to see the hurricane deck lined with sailors covering the pier with rifles. Soapy, however, hadn't seen them yet. He and his gang were pushing their way through the wharf's crowd towards Wood. As they tried to corner the Mounties, Soapy and Wood came face to face. Both men had their guns ready, and it looked as though those guns would be blazing soon. Nevertheless, Wood remained calm and unflappable. Then Soapy, seeing the armed escort of sailors marching onto the wharf and another squad lined up on the ship's deck, called off the attack. As Wood passed Soapy and headed towards the gangplank of the *Tartar*, Soapy smiled at him and said, "Why not hang around and visit Skagway for a day or two?"

Wood gave a wry smile and declined. It would be the last

time he saw Soapy. A month later, Soapy put a derringer in his sleeve, a .45 Colt revolver in his pocket and a Winchester .30/30 on his shoulder and then went to confront a vigilante group that was meeting to discuss him. Before heading off, Soapy told an associate, "I am about due to kill a man and I have lived long enough myself anyway." When four guards barred his way to the meeting, Soapy unslung the Winchester from his shoulder and said to one of them, Frank Reid, "Damn you, Reid … you're at the bottom of all my troubles. I should have got rid of you three months ago."

The two men were standing close when Smith levelled his Winchester at Reid's head and Reid reached for his own six-gun. Moments later, Soapy was dead and Reid was mortally wounded. Both were buried at the same cemetery, just a few feet away from each other.

CHAPTER

4

Pushing into
the Arctic

AFTER THE FRENZIED DAYS OF the Klondike Gold
Rush, policing in the Yukon settled down to conduct-
ing regular patrols, investigating crime, managing
drunks, guarding prisoners and checking on prospectors
and trappers. Mounties also helped other government
agencies collect fees, issue licences, collect customs
and taxes, take censuses and handle mail at isolated
posts.

In 1903, the NWMP began to push deeper into the
Canadian North with two historic patrols that brought law
and order beyond the Arctic Circle, reaffirming Canadian
sovereignty over the area. One patrol would sail to
Hudson's Bay to establish an NWMP presence in the eastern

Arctic. Led by the unflappable Inspector J.D. Moodie, this 16-man patrol left Halifax on the SS *Neptune* on August 22 and by that fall had successfully built a detachment at Fullerton. The other patrol, headed by Superintendent Charles Constantine, would go deep into the western Arctic and subarctic via the Mackenzie River system.

The Western Arctic Patrol

In May 1903, Superintendent Constantine left Fort Saskatchewan with 34-year-old Sergeant Frank Fitzgerald, four constables (S.S. Munroe, F.D. Sutherland, R.H. Walker and John Galpin) and Special Constable Joseph Belrose to bring Mountie authority to the Mackenzie River area and the Arctic. They would be establishing a new police detachment at Fort McPherson and perhaps another on Herschel Island, in response to complaints that American whaling ships were using the island as a winter stopover and demoralizing the Inuit population with alcohol. Constantine assigned Fitzgerald the command of both the Fort McPherson and Herschel Island posts.

It took the men two months to reach their destination. They canoed up the Athabasca and Slave Rivers, portaged 25 kilometres over difficult terrain to Fort Smith, sailed the Mackenzie River on the SS *Wrigley* and in mid-July crossed the Arctic Circle to begin the last leg of their journey to Fort McPherson.

By all accounts, Fort McPherson was a desolate place in

1903. Located on the Peel River, about 50 kilometres above the junction of the Peel and Mackenzie Rivers, it stood just under 160 kilometres from the Arctic Ocean. The Hudson's Bay Company had five buildings at Fort McPherson, and all except one were rundown. There was also a church, a missionary house and a few Native huts. Dogs—after whom no one cleaned up—overran much of the village. Even in July, the place was cold and inhospitable.

To house the NWMP's first post above the Arctic Circle, Constantine rented several vacant buildings for $45 for three months. He then returned to Fort Saskatchewan, but before leaving, gave Sergeant Fitzgerald two orders. The first order was to go to Herschel Island as soon as possible to see if the American whalers or Inuit were still there and to establish a police detachment on the island. The second was to develop the best all-Canadian route from Fort McPherson to Dawson City so that Fitzgerald and his men could communicate with the outside world.

Constantine understood first-hand the stresses and emotional strain that came from being stationed so far away from civilization. When he left Fitzgerald and the men at Fort McPherson he wrote, "I felt for the men standing on the beach as I well remember the feeling that came over our party in the Yukon in 1895 when the last steamer left, being cut off from the outside world for a year at least, strangers in a strange land."

But the detachment's new commander was also a

veteran of such service. Fitzgerald had joined the NWMP at the age of 18 and 9 years later had been part of the famous 14-month patrol, headed by Inspector J.D. Moodie, that had blazed the first all-Canadian overland route from Edmonton to the Klondike.

Within two weeks of arriving at Fort McPherson, Fitzgerald, Sutherland, and their interpreter, Thompson, sailed to Herschel Island on a mission whaleboat. It took them 10 days to make the 420-kilometre trip, at one point battling 130-kilometre-per-hour winds on the Arctic Ocean.

Herschel Island is a barren piece of rock about 20 kilometres long and 5 kilometres wide. Sir John Franklin had sighted the island on July 17, 1826, and had named it after Sir John Hersch, a well-known British chemist and astronomer and a personal friend of Franklin's. Devoid of any trees or brush, the island was dotted instead with six warehouse buildings when Fitzgerald and his men came upon it. Four were owned by the Pacific Steam Whaling Company, one was built circa 1894 by Captain James McKenna of the whaler *Charles Hanson* and one was owned by an Anglican mission. There were also 15 sod houses there, which Fitzgerald later wrote were "owned by the Pacific Steam Whaling Company and are used in the winter by the officers of the whalers who nearly all keep a native woman in the winter."

During 1893–94, when whaling was at its peak, Herschel Island had been the largest community in the Yukon, with an estimated population of 1,500. Now, almost 10 years later, Fitzgerald discovered that the American whalers had not abandoned the island. The previous winter, two whaling ships—*Narwhal* and *Olga*—with a total of 67 men had wintered there. And a mere week after Fitzgerald, Sutherland and Thompson reached the island, six ships of the American whaling fleet of the Pacific Steam Whaling Company arrived: the *Alexander, Thrasher, Bowhead, Belvedere, Baylies* and *Beluga*. Onboard were over 250 men, looking to spend the winter there.

Whaling was big business—the bone alone from a mature whale was worth $10,000 in the 1890s. In a 17-year span (1889–1906), mostly foreign whalers took around 1,345 whales out of Canadian waters while using Canada as a base of operations.

As the whaling captains came ashore on Herschel Island, the two NWMP in their scarlet tunics were waiting on the beach. Fitzgerald personally greeted each one, as Sutherland stood to the side. Politely but bluntly, Fitzgerald informed the whalers that Canadian law must be obeyed, warned them that they could no longer supply liquor to the Inuit and explained that, in the future, Canadian customs duties would be collected on all goods landed on the island. The crusty captains looked concerned, glancing at the scarlet tunics and the Union Jack now flying above the mission hut. But surprisingly they agreed amicably to Canadian police authority.

A few weeks later, Fitzgerald and Sutherland made a

harrowing return to Fort McPherson. A two-day storm broke their boat into pieces, forcing them to camp on a sandspit. They were able to hire a passing Inuit whaleboat to take them the rest of the way, but salt water had ruined most of their provisions and they were left only with a little flour, a few rabbits and falling snow for water.

Soon after arriving at Fort McPherson, Fitzgerald prepared to return to Herschel Island. With the whalers overwintering on the island, he felt he had to be there to keep an eye on them. He had already made arrangements with the Anglican missionary on Herschel Island, Reverend C.E. Whittaker, to transport him and his supplies back to the island on the missionary's boat.

Once he was back on Herschel Island, Fitzgerald bought two sod houses and a storehouse for winter quarters and purchased five tons of coal ($20 per ton) from the SS *Baylies*, one of the whalers wintering there. He was based on the island for several years.

Fitzgerald handled several important cases and situations during his time on Herschel Island, but none was as controversial internationally as his confrontation with famous explorer-anthropologist Vilhjalmur Stefansson in 1908. Stefansson—who had been sent north by the Canadian government and the American Museum of Natural History to study the Inuit—was travelling light and had forgotten to include matches in his expedition supplies. Without matches, Stefansson felt it would be difficult for his party, which included Dr. R.M. Anderson and nine Inuit, to make it through the winter. Captain James Wing of the *Karluk* supplied Stefansson with 1,000 matches, which suited him fine, but there were smokers in his group who refused to continue their Arctic journey until they had more matches. Stefansson decided to wait and buy matches from the supply ships expected to arrive shortly at Herschel Island, but they never arrived.

Desperate, Stefansson pleaded with Fitzgerald to give him more matches. Fitzgerald staunchly refused, trying to force Stefansson to abandon his winter expedition. The officer felt Stefansson was ill prepared for his Arctic expedition, as his party carried no food supplies and expected to live off the land—an action that could put them in a starvation situation, requiring rescue. Fitzgerald promised the men a cabin and supplies if they remained on Herschel Island for the winter, but said that if they chose to leave, he would not provide them with matches. Stefansson refused the wintering offer. A few days later, his expedition sailed west to Point Barrow, where the men bought matches and—heeding Fitzgerald's warnings—enough food to last the whole winter. In the meantime, the confrontation had become news around the world, and many saw Fitzgerald in a negative light. His superiors, however, reviewed the case and supported his actions.

Although Fitzgerald was one of the true "Northern Men" of the Mounties, the dark winter and cold isolation of the Arctic still did affect him. In 1909 he wrote, "When there are no ships wintering at Herschel Island, I think that it is one of the most lonesome places on earth. There is no place one can go, except to visit a few hungry natives, and there is no white man to visit nearer than 180 miles."

Despite this isolation, Fitzgerald nevertheless managed to find romance while stationed at the island's lonely police post. He fell in love with an Inuit woman named Lena Oonalina, but his superiors refused to grant them permission to marry. In the summer of 1909, he and Lena had a child named Annie who was baptized by the island's Anglican minister, Reverend W.H. Fry. Annie was born with a disability and died at Hay River when she was 18.

At Fort McPherson and Herschel Island, Fitzgerald had successfully completed what he was ordered to do—establish the world's most northerly police post. But soon he would face many more obstacles.

The Lost Patrol
On December 21, 1910, before Inspector Fitzgerald headed out on his patrol between Dawson City and Fort McPherson —a distance of 800 kilometres—he shook hands with Corporal Somers of the Fort McPherson detachment and waved goodbye to John Firth, the long-time HBC post manager. It was just another routine winter patrol; Fitzgerald had completed the Dawson–Fort McPherson winter patrol on four previous occasions. But this time was different. This

year the patrol would go from Fort McPherson to Dawson instead of the other way around.

Leaving Fort McPherson with Fitzgerald were Constable George Frances Kinney (27), Constable Richard O'Hara Taylor (28) and Special Constable Sam Carter (41), an ex-Mountie of 21 years. The men carried with them over 600 pounds of supplies per sled, including bacon, salt, milk in tins, flour, dried fruit, beans, coffee and tea, baking powder and sugar. Later, some would suggest that the party's supplies had been too light for such a long trek and that perhaps Fitzgerald had been trying to set a record time for the journey.

When the patrol set out on December 21, the weather conditions were terrible, with ice fog and heavy snows. On Christmas Day, there was heavy mist and a northwest wind, with temperatures hovering around –35°C. The patrol camped with several Native families and Fitzgerald hired one of the men, Esau, to break trail and guide the party across the portage to the Peel River. On New Year's Day, Fitzgerald paid Esau $24 for his services and they parted company.

The cold continued, and so did the heavy snowstorms. On January 8, the temperature dipped to –55°C with strong headwinds—it was so cold that moisture from the men's breath condensed and froze to form thin shreds of ice on their faces. Four days later, still plagued by frigid conditions, Fitzgerald recorded in his diary that they were lost.

Days passed, and still the party could not find their way. As the gale-force winds continued to blow, desperation began to set in among the men. On January 17, Fitzgerald wrote the following in his diary:

> Carter is completely lost and does not know one river from another. We have only 10 pounds of flour and 8 pounds of bacon and some dried fish. My last hope is gone, and the only thing I can do is to return, and kill some of our dogs to feed the others and ourselves, unless we can meet some Indians.
>
> We have now been a week looking for a river to take us over the divide, but there are dozens of rivers and I am at a loss.

The next day, January 18, with their food almost gone, the men started to head back to Fort McPherson. That night, they were forced to kill their first dog, which they fed to the remaining dogs. The men continued to eat small pieces of bannock and dried fish. On January 19, they killed their second dog.

Although the temperature warmed up to −29°C, the weather got worse, and the men, almost out of their supplies, were forced to eat dog meat. By January 22, the temperature had fallen to −53°C, and a heavy mist and gale descended once again.

Two days later, it was still bitterly cold with strong

winds, but the starving, exhausted men continued on. They headed down the Wind River and were surprised to come upon some open water. As the group climbed the riverbank to bypass the open stretch, Constable Taylor fell into the icy waters up to his waist, and Special Constable Carter fell in to his hips. Quickly, a campfire was made to warm up the two men.

By February 1, 8 of the 15 sled dogs had been killed for food. On February 5, Fitzgerald wrote in his diary:

> Forty-eight below. Saturday, February 5. – Fine with strong S.E. wind. Left camp at 7:15 a.m.; nooned one hour, and camped about eight miles further down. Just after noon I broke through the ice and had to make fire; found one foot slightly frozen. Killed another dog to-night; have only five dogs now, and can only go a few miles a day; everybody breaking out on the body and skin peeling off. Eight miles.

This would be his last journal entry.

Back in Dawson City, authorities became concerned when the Native guide, Esau, arrived at the detachment on February 20 and told Superintendent Snyder that he'd met Fitzgerald and the patrol on Trail River back on December 26 and, after travelling together for a few days, had left them on January 1. Esau then reported that the group had missed the regular patrol route.

Though the party was long overdue, there hadn't been much cause for concern because everyone knew of Fitzgerald's expertise in northern travel and survival. However, Esau's report worried Superintendent Snyder, and he started to make plans to look for the missing men.

On February 28, 1911, a search party was sent out from Dawson City. It included Corporal William John "Jack" Dempster (for whom the Dempster Highway was later named), Constable J.F. Fyfe, ex-constable F. Turner and Native guide Charles Stewart.

Despite bad weather, the search party covered the patrol's route in record time. On March 12, Dempster found one of Fitzgerald's night camps. The next day, he passed a few more, only six kilometres apart. On March 19, while at Colin Vitisk's cabin on the Peel River, Dempster found some packages on the roof beam. When Stewart pulled them off the beam, they discovered the packages consisted of 30 pounds of Fitzgerald's dispatch and mailbags.

Two days later, Dempster found an abandoned toboggan and two sets of dog harnesses on the ice. Then he saw something even more ominous—a blue kerchief waving in the wind, tied to a willow on the riverbank. He climbed up the bank, walked through some willows, found a small open camp and, in the clearing, discovered the bodies of Constables Kinney and Taylor, lying next to each other. Apparently, Kinney had died first, as he was laid out with both hands folded neatly across his chest. Next to him was the twisted body of Taylor, who had shot himself with a .30/30 rifle sometime after Kinney's death. The search party covered the men with brush and continued on down the Peel River, still hoping that Fitzgerald and Carter were alive.

The following morning, 16 kilometres further down the river, the search party followed a faint trail that went up to the riverbank. They found a pair of snowshoes and then, in a stand of timber only 40 kilometres from Fort McPherson, they found the bodies of Fitzgerald and Carter. Fitzgerald had died after Carter, and the evidence indicated that he'd dragged Carter's body three metres from their campfire, crossed his arms over his body and placed a handkerchief over his face. Fitzgerald's body was found lying beside the campfire, with two thin blankets pulled around him.

The search party covered the men's bodies with brush and then raced to Fort McPherson with the tragic news. A few days later, Corporal Somers, with Special Constable Jimmie Husky and HBC agent Peter Ross, retrieved the bodies and brought them back to Fort McPherson for burial.

Reverend C.E. Whittaker—who had lived on Herschel Island and spent time with Fitzgerald—helped make the four coffins. Then, on March 28, the four men were buried in Fort McPherson with full military honours in the churchyard of the Church of England mission.

Continuing the Road to Nowhere

In 1897, the Canadian government gave Inspector Moodie

the order to blaze and survey an all-Canadian backdoor route to the Yukon. Eight years later, in 1905, the government issued a similar order when it demanded the RNWMP (the newly added "R" stood for "Royal," the prefix given by King Edward VII in 1904) undertake to build a pack trail from the Peace River to the Yukon.

Why the government wanted the Yukon trail project reopened in 1905 is not clear. The gold rush was over, and population in the North had waned considerably. It was possible that members of the government were still concerned that the Americans would seize the Yukon. (At one point, Canadian authorities even sent machine guns to be mounted in the Yukon for defence against any American invasion.) Whatever the case, it wasn't up to the Mounties to question the reasons and motives—it was simply up to them to carry out the order.

The RNWMP were told to build a trail for pack ponies, but to construct it in such a way that it could be widened later for a wagon trail. The route chosen would be based on the one first suggested by Moodie after his 1897–98 survey patrol. Along with constructing the road, the Mounties were tasked with brushing all the muskeg, bridging rivers, erecting mileposts and building rest houses at intervals of 48 kilometres for future travellers.

Once again, it looked like a full construction road-building crew that marched out from the RNWMP detachment at Fort Saskatchewan on March 17, 1905, headed for Fort St.

John—917 kilometres away. Leading the expedition to build the Peace River–Yukon trail was the man who had first made the recommendation in 1897, Superintendent Charles Constantine. Accompanying him were Inspector Richard, 30 non-commissioned officers and constables and 60 horses. They were to build a 2.6-metre-wide trail stretching 1,200 kilometres from Fort St. John to Teslin, in the Yukon. And Constantine was told that "the work must be rushed."

The party arrived at Fort St. John on June 1 and spent the first two weeks there constructing a small police barracks for their summer and winter quarters. The horses, however, would winter up the road with a few men to take care of them. To ensure there was forage, some Mounties became haymakers, providing 140 tons of hay for the first winter.

On June 15, the men began construction of the Peace River–Yukon trail. They built bridges across streams, graded steep banks and hacked through standing timber and extensive windfalls. They climbed over mountain passes, down into valleys and through swampy lowlands. It was painstaking and exhausting work. By September 25, just over three months later, they had finished building 150 kilometres of highway and were getting ready for winter.

It was a bitterly cold first winter for the men at Fort St. John, made particularly hard because the steamer carrying their supplies had been unable to get these supplies to them. To obtain some of the more vital provisions, the Mounties drove one-horse sleighs over the difficult mountain trails, but the horses became so exhausted that they had to be helped up in the mornings. Clothing supplies were not considered vital and were therefore not replenished. This forced some of the Mounties to wear moose hides and flour sacks in place of their tattered clothes.

By August 1906, another 215 kilometres of trail had been built, and the pack route now reached Fort Grahame (320 kilometres from Fort St. John). However, the men had been forced to work under horrible rainy conditions. Their hay crop was ruined and 13 horses had died. Then, as if road building wasn't difficult enough, the exhausted men had to build a small barracks at Fort Grahame for winter quarters, complete with horse corrals.

By spring 1907, the men were once again building their road, and by September 1907, they had added another 241 kilometres to the trail, bringing the completed total to 575 kilometres from Fort St. John. That autumn, Commissioner Perry inspected the trail and declared it was a good one that could be converted to a wagon trail.

With the most difficult part of the trail now built, the goal of completion was within sight. After three seasons of exhausting work, the all-Canadian backdoor route to the Yukon would soon be opened.

It was at this point that the federal government ordered Commissioner Perry to ask the British Columbia government to assist in some of the road-building expenses. The

BC government, however, refused to share the costs. As a result, the federal government decided to withdraw the RNWMP and abandon the project.

To the bitter disappointment of the Mounties, the 575 kilometres of the Peace River–Yukon trail, which had taken three years of their lives to build, became an abandoned road to nowhere.

One Last Effort

Two long and difficult Mountie patrols, totalling over four years of hard work, had failed to complete a road to the Yukon from Peace River Country in Alberta. In 1910, a third road-building patrol was assigned to the Road to Nowhere.

This time, 34-year-old Sergeant John "Jock" Darling would lead the trail builders, accompanied by 27-year-old Constable Robert Cranford Bowen and 21-year-old Constable Armand St. Laurent. Their task was to follow and clear the trail built 5 years earlier by Constantine's party and originally blazed 13 years earlier by Moodie's group. Unlike the other two patrols, Darling's group was directed to continue to Whitehorse, via Telegraph Creek and Atlin.

The men left Athabasca Landing on May 4, 1910, with saddle horses, wagon teams and 11 packhorses. Problems plagued their trek right from the start, when a wagon turned over twice and had to be reloaded. After that, it was just one hardship after another. The group had to deal with bush fires, wagon teams that couldn't keep up with the packhorses and a brutal trail that injured their horses. Then they had to battle snow, rain and thunderstorms. They were forced to recover wagons stuck in muskeg, build bridges across swollen rivers and fight hordes of mosquitoes and black flies that made life almost unbearable. On June 5, a month after they first set out, they arrived at Lake St. John in British Columbia. The next 950 kilometres were the most difficult. Challenges included deep, snow-covered valleys, high mountain trails obscured by snow, regular deadfalls, rotten bridges and horse stampedes.

One of the hardest days of the expedition was June 23, when the party had to cross the Osipaka River in the rain. At 5 a.m. the men started to build a raft large enough to take wagons and supplies across the river, but they used too much green, heavy timber and had to rebuild it. It took eight raft trips to get all the equipment across the river, and then the men had to swim the horses over.

When they arrived at Atlin on October 5, they still had 200 kilometres to go to Whitehorse, but the group decided they'd had enough of the trekking through bush and hopped on the steamer *Atlin* to complete their journey. During the five-month trek, the Darling Patrol had covered 2,700 kilometres.

Three times the Mounties had successfully tackled incredible challenges while trying to build a trail to the Yukon, and three times the wilderness reclaimed it. The Road to Nowhere was never finished.

5

Crazy Exploits
in the North Country

THOSE WHO HAVE EXPERIENCED THE isolation and long darkness of a winter in the North often insist that unless a person has lived through such a winter, he or she cannot understand how these conditions can play with one's mind. In his book *Ellesmere Island, A Mountie in the High Arctic*, retired RCMP sergeant Edgar Kuhn describes his own efforts to overcome the desolation of a Northern winter: "It is clear that the second sunless winter was having a dire effect on my very human mind. I wouldn't have admitted it, but obviously some kind of unreasoning depression was taking possession of my soul, a very hopeless feeling. It could only be counteracted with exercise and diversion ... I had to push myself continually just to maintain a sane existence."

Old-timers called it "cabin fever" and knew its dark side could push even the strongest-willed man over the edge into insanity. Some became so violently insane that they were more than capable of killing themselves or others.

One of the only ways to deal with extreme cabin fever was to get the sufferer out of his isolated environment and into a medical facility for treatment. The task of transporting these desperately ill people went to the Mounties, and they were soon performing this duty often enough that officers gave a name to the nightmare journeys—lunatic patrols. In one year alone, over 40 such patrols were made between Dawson City and Whitehorse. As R.C. Fetherstonhaugh wrote in *The Royal Canadian Mounted Police*, the tales of these patrols often "surpass in horror the grimmest of macabre fiction."

The lunatic patrol carried out by Sergeant Field, stationed at Fort Chipewyan in 1902, is one example of what a Mountie was forced to endure during one of these trying runs. Field had just returned from a long mid-winter patrol when he received a message about a man who had gone "violently insane" in Hay River, 560 kilometres north of Fort Chipewyan. The only way to get to Hay River was by dog team, so Field hooked up his dogs again and set off with a Native interpreter for the small community on Great Slave Lake. Field knew if the man in question had indeed gone insane, he would have to bring him out by dogsled to get medical attention.

As the sergeant and his interpreter mushed to Hay River, Field hoped the man's illness would be mild enough that it could be treated at Fort Chipewyan, which was located at the northwestern end of Lake Athabasca, about 160 kilometres from the current Northwest Territories border. However, if the man's illness was as severe as the message had implied, a difficult journey lay ahead for both the Mountie and the sick man.

When Field got to Hay River, things didn't look good—the man was so deeply affected that he had become a raving maniac, snarling like a wild animal and glaring murderously at anyone who came near him. Field had no choice but take him on a 1,200-kilometre journey to Fort Saskatchewan for medical treatment.

For the next six weeks, Sergeant Field protected and cared for his charge. He fed and exercised him, guarded him every hour from frostbite in the freezing temperatures and blinding blizzards, and slept beside him—when he could get sleep. At all times, Field was careful to keep weapons out of the man's reach. And there was no rest emotionally or mentally while on the lunatic patrol. By day, Field listened to the man's mad ravings and at night to his screams.

Happily for Field, once his small group reached Fort Saskatchewan, medical authorities took over. His taxing job done, Field turned around and headed back to his regular duties at Fort Chipewyan.

While Sergeant Field had been able to return to his post

relatively unscathed by his lunatic patrol, sometimes the stress of such a patrol could break the health of even the strongest Mounties—Mounties like Constable Albert Pedley. Also stationed at Fort Chipewyan, British-born Pedley was 22 years old when he joined the NWMP on April 18, 1900. After spending three months in Regina, he was stationed at Fort Saskatchewan (about 32 kilometres east of Edmonton) before being posted to Fort Chipewyan.

Pedley's lunatic patrol began on December 17, 1904, when he and an interpreter, Special Constable Damies, left Fort Chipewyan with two dog teams to bring an "insane" missionary to a hospital in Fort Saskatchewan, 645 kilometres away. Pedley put the man in a sleeping bag, covered him in thick fur and strapped him onto the police dogsled. For the next five days, Pedley and the interpreter ran behind the sleds, through slush and water up to their knees. It was a brutal, demanding trek.

The temperature was so bitterly cold throughout the patrol that when the men arrived at Fort McKay five days later, Pedley purchased moccasins for the missionary's frozen feet. The weather continued to worsen, with the temperature plunging to –50°C. Suddenly, a vicious blizzard swept in and it became too dangerous for the patrol to continue. To protect the dogs, Pedley dug them a trench and used the overturned sled as their windbreak. Then, keeping the missionary in the sleeping bag, Pedley and the interpreter lashed him to a tree so that the forceful winds would not blow him away. After that, they climbed into their own sleeping bags and lashed themselves to the trees as well.

The storm lasted for 48 hours. Once it was over, the small group pushed south to wooded country that was more sheltered, but this area contained an abundance of timber wolves. Each evening, Pedley lit a huge fire as protection against attack from the hungry wolves; throughout the night, he would get up and keep the fire going.

During all these tribulations, the insane missionary constantly raved. Twice when he refused to eat, Pedley freed him to give him exercise. Both times, he attempted to flee into the wilderness. The second time, he waited until Pedley's arms were full of wood for the campfire and then bolted to freedom. Pedley chased him through the snow for almost a kilometre before he overtook him, tied his hands and feet and then, facing a bitter wind, carried the man back to the camp.

The patrol arrived at Lac La Biche on New Year's Eve, just in time for some celebrating. Special Constable Damies attended a dance, but at 10 p.m. he raced back to get Pedley because a fight had broken out. The Mountie arrived on the scene, quickly arrested a drunken troublemaker and then went looking for the rest of the liquor. He searched two houses in the community, found brandy and whisky, and arrested two more men. Now he had a total of four people in his custody, and before they could continue, another sled and dog team had to be hired. The group finally left

Lac La Biche on January 2, heading for Fort Saskatchewan. Pedley intended to drop off the three drunks to be tried at the nearest magistrate.

Two days later, the grumbling group arrived at Saddle Lake and Pedley laid information against the Lac La Biche prisoners before a justice of the peace. The next day, the three men were convicted and Pedley continued on to Fort Saskatchewan with Special Constable Damies and their insane charge.

The exhausted patrol arrived in Fort Saskatchewan on January 7, 1905. Pedley handed over the missionary, but while the Mountie's gruelling journey was over, that was not the case for the seriously ill missionary. The Mountie detachment at Fort Saskatchewan transported the man to the RNWMP guardroom at Calgary for further assessment by RNWMP assistant surgeon Rouleau, who later reported, "He was badly frozen about his feet, and the exposure to the cold had caused paralysis of the tongue for several days. Every care and attention was given him at the hospital with the result that he was discharged on February 29 with the loss only of the first joint of a big toe. His mind and speech were as good as ever."

But things didn't go as well for Pedley. Before leaving Fort Saskatchewan, Pedley commuted for the next month to Edmonton for dental work. On February 8, he left the fort with Constable George D. Ferris and Special Constable Cecil E. Denny (later to become Sir Cecil E. Denny).

Commissioner Aylesworth Bowen Perry wrote in his 1905 Annual Report, "Constable Pedley commenced his return trip to Fort Chipewyan. When he left Fort Saskatchewan he was apparently in good health, but at Lac La Biche he went violently insane as a result of the hardships of the trip and his anxiety for the safety of his charge."

The others had noticed that his health had begun to deteriorate after a few days on the trail. Pedley didn't eat or sleep for five days and then, on February 13, he became violently ill. His condition continued to worsen so dramatically that it was decided to bring him back to Fort Saskatchewan.

Pedley was transferred to a hospital in Brandon, Manitoba, where he stayed until October 4. After a further three months' leave, he returned to active duty in Regina in early 1906. He was promoted to corporal and sergeant before retiring in 1924. His ordeal received wide publicity and later became the basis for a 1952 Hollywood movie called *The Wild North*, with the role of Pedley played by Wendell Corey.

Peace River Sleuth

Policing the rugged northern country was demanding work, and because the land was so vast and sparsely populated, sometimes a crime could go undetected. In 1904, a Utah trader by the name of Charles King almost got away with murder in Peace River Country. He was foiled, however, by a dog, the keen observation of a young Native boy and the methodical detective work of a Mountie named Kristjan Fjeldsted "Andy" Anderson.

Born in Iceland in 1866, Anderson immigrated to Canada in 1887. After working briefly on railway construction, he joined the NWMP in Regina on August 19, 1889. He spent most of his career in the north, serving in Maple Creek, Fort Saskatchewan, Lesser Slave Lake and Grouard. A big man with a powerful physique, a hard-featured face and piercing blue eyes, his commanding presence, devotion to duty and bold exploits made him into a northern legend. Old-timers from Athabasca Landing to the Rockies said Anderson was "the toughest policeman they had ever known."

In August 1904, Staff Sergeant Anderson was posted at Lesser Slave Lake when Utah trapper Charles King and well-to-do British expatriate Edward Hayward left Edmonton as partners headed for Peace River Country with an outfit of packhorses and supplies for a year of trapping and hunting. The pair travelled over the Swan Hills Trail to Lesser Slave Lake and on September 17 camped on the reserve at Sucker Creek. There, they socialized with the Sucker Creek peoples and others who dropped in to see them. The next day, King closed up camp alone and left with the outfit, explaining that Hayward had already gone on to Sturgeon Lake.

But Chief Moos Toos of the Sucker Creek Reserve was suspicious, as he and others had heard a gunshot the night before. Someone on the reserve had also seen King stoking a big fire.

A few days later, Moos Toos was travelling with Staff Sergeant Anderson and confided to the Mountie that two white men had recently camped on the Sucker Creek Reserve, but that only one had left. He told Anderson that after King had left, the women from his band had gone to the campsite to look for discarded items that might be useful and noticed that the campfire had been unusually large. One of the women looked above the fire and noticed layers of fat on the underside of some tree leaves. This woman told Moos Toos, "Someone burned flesh at that fire."

Added to these strange circumstances was a young Native boy's observation that for some reason the men's dog had refused to follow the remaining white man, staying close to the campsite instead.

Something seemed wrong, said Moos Toos. Staff Sergeant Anderson and Constable Lowe agreed. Together with the chief, they went to the men's campsite to investigate. Raking the ashes, they found buttons and bone fragments. Then, in a hole under the ashes, they discovered bits of flesh and what looked like a human heart. Nearby, Moos Toos and his people waded barefoot in the slough; on the muddy bottom they found a camp kettle, a pair of boots stuffed with various articles, including rags, and the remainder of a broken needle.

Anderson and Lowe rode after King and arrested him, even though they had no body or any solid evidence that could convict him in court. Hoping to find anything that would definitely indicate Hayward had been murdered there, Anderson then returned to the campfire site. As he sifted through the ashes once again, he kept glancing at the slough. Suspecting that it held more evidence, he hired the Natives to dig a kilometre-long ditch to divert and drain the slough into Sucker Creek.

Just as Anderson thought, the slough held several valuable clues: buttons, a belt buckle, a pocketknife and bones later identified as spinal vertebrae with a bullet embedded in them (the bullet was the same calibre as King's revolver). Of particular interest was a case designed to hold English sovereigns, engraved with the name of its English manufacturer. Anderson traced the case back to England and discovered that Hayward's father had purchased it for his son to take with him to northern Canada. The clues were neatly falling into place—even though there was no body.

Charles King was tried for murder in Edmonton in February 1905. During the lengthy and expensive trial, Hayward's brother travelled from England to identify the sovereign case as belonging to his brother (police paid for his fare and expenses); a pathologist confirmed the charred bone, flesh and heart as human; and witnesses testified that they had seen King and Hayward leave Edmonton together as partners. No body was ever found, but Anderson had so persistently and methodically built such a strong case on circumstantial evidence that King was found guilty and sentenced to hang.

But then came a snag. On a technicality, King's lawyer won a new trial for his client. Another court date was set, the witnesses all returned and the same evidence was presented. Once again, King was convicted and sentenced to death. He was executed on September 30, 1905, at Fort Saskatchewan.

Head in a Sack

Mounties in remote locations, often alone in responding to a situation, were sometimes forced to improvise when carrying out their policing duties. One of the strangest tales of Mountie improvisation centres on Staff Sergeant Andy Anderson. Known for his unorthodox methods of policing, Anderson once transported a severed head from the Peace River area to a courtroom in Kamloops.

The story began in 1910, when two trappers named Coleman and Trotter quarrelled during the winter. The men had been living together for the season at Coleman Creek, on the Pouce Coupe prairie. As the tale goes, Coleman became irritated and angry with Trotter, who was hollowing out a log for a water trough with a hammer and chisel. Some say Coleman may have gone over the edge with cabin fever, as he suddenly reached for his gun off the wall. When Trotter saw that Coleman was reaching for his weapon, he slammed his partner's head hard with the hammer. The blow caused Coleman to fall into the roaring fire in the cabin's fireplace, and his body was partly burned.

Terrified, Trotter ran to seek help from a storeowner named Tremblay, about 16 kilometres away. The men returned to find Coleman dead. Without moving Coleman's body, and leaving Trotter in charge of his store, Tremblay sped by dog team to report the death to Anderson and the RNWMP detachment at Peace River, over 250 kilometres away.

Once back at Coleman Creek, Anderson checked the murder site and arrested Trotter for the killing. He then faced the task of bringing both the accused and the evidence to Kamloops, the nearest place where a murder trial could be held. Trotter would either be convicted of murder or acquitted on self-defence—either way, Anderson needed to bring to court evidence of the attack.

But there was a problem with the evidence: the victim's body was now frozen stiff. Anderson considered taking the body by dog team to the railway station on the Athabasca River at Mirror Landing, east of Lesser Slave Lake, but figured it would be very difficult to transport the body by train via Edmonton to the court in Kamloops. Writer Dorothea Calverley describes what Anderson did next in her book *Policing the Peace Country*: "The only part of the body that bore evidence (of an attack) was the head, so the resourceful Mountie chopped it off, put it in a pail, put that in a gunny sack and started off with his grisly burden."

There were some difficult moments during the dogsled journey with the severed head (which was wrapped in paper and packed with hay around it) and the accused. In the evenings, to prevent animals from getting at the head,

Anderson had to hang the gunny sack high in the trees. One night, however, he almost lost the head when he hung the bag a little too low and the sled dogs pulled it down. They were just about to destroy the evidence when Trotter woke Anderson up in time to rescue the head.

On another occasion, the officer and his prisoner battled a terrible snowstorm. Both were exhausted, but when Anderson wanted to rest, it was Trotter who convinced the sergeant to keep going—if he stopped to rest, he would freeze to death. Trotter saved Anderson's life by keeping him moving until the blizzard was over.

At the Kamloops trial, Anderson showed the severed head as evidence, but didn't make a strong case for murder. Calverley writes that Anderson asked the judge, "Sir, what do you think was the cause of death?"

The judge replied, "Decapitation, of course!"

Trotter told the judge and jury that he killed Coleman in self-defence, and he was soon acquitted of murder. When the trial ended, Anderson and Trotter headed back together to Peace River Country.

After a colourful career, Anderson retired from the RCMP on January 1, 1921. He died in January 1949. A memorial article in the *RCMP Quarterly* noted that with Anderson's passing, the Force had lost "another who did so much to carve out of the wilderness the foundation and traditions of the Force ... His deeds are indeed his monument."

6

Breaking Boundaries

AS ONE OF THE WORLD's largest police forces, and one of the oldest, there isn't much the Mounties haven't seen or dealt with in carrying out their diverse range of duties. The early policing pioneers of the RCMP broke boundaries to establish law and order. Sometimes they crossed geographical borders, sometimes physical, social or systemic barriers, and sometimes they pushed their own personal boundaries. Whatever the case, the traditional breaking of boundaries was done in compliance with the Mounties' official motto, *Maintiens le droit*, or "Maintain the Right."

Rescuing a Wizard

In 1902, the border between the Yukon and Alaska was

still in dispute, and rumours persisted that the Americans were ready to invade and seize the Yukon. Senior police and government officials took the threats so seriously that Superintendent Constantine returned to the Yukon to prepare for the American invasion. He developed a defence strategy that included drawing up lists of available military personnel in the territory and ordering two machine guns.

It was a tense time, and the NWMP were careful not to start any international incidents. But on February 1, 1902, three NWMP constables stationed along the boundary line were faced with one of their strangest cases in Yukon policing, one that would involve an illegal rescue mission across the American border.

It was nighttime when a highly agitated missionary posted in the village of Kluk-wan, a few kilometres away in Alaska, stormed into the NWMP border detachment at Wells. The officer in charge, Constable A.G. Leeson, listened carefully as the missionary, Mr. Sellon, told of a young Chilcat boy being tortured by the band's elders for allegedly practising witchcraft.

The missionary begged for help. He said that the boy, named Kodik, would soon die if he wasn't rescued. But it was a touchy political situation for Constable Leeson. He couldn't just rush over to Alaska to save the boy—as a Canadian police officer he had no authority on American soil.

Still, wanting to do something, Leeson came up with a two-step solution. First, he loudly proclaimed that as an

NWMP constable he was powerless do anything. Next he explained in a quieter voice that if he crossed the boundary line as a "private person," carrying his own pistol, he could help save the boy.

Two other constables—R. Brown and C.P. Simpson—volunteered to join him in the mission. Quickly, they changed into civilian clothes, packed their own revolvers, along with a pick, a shovel and an axe, and then set out. They crossed into American territory and headed for the north bank of the Chilkat River in Alaska.

Mr. Sellon led them to an empty house in the village, but a quick search found no sign of the boy. As they were about to leave, one of the officers noticed an oddly placed woodpile on the outer porch. He shifted the firewood, lifted two loose floor planks underneath and found an ice-coated hole with the barely conscious boy doubled up inside. The temperature had been hovering around -40°C.

The men wrapped the boy in blankets, carried him to the missionary's house and revived him. Mr. Sellon explained that the elders had accused Kodik of practising witchcraft to cause the illness of Chief Yakesha. The elders had then decided that the boy must die, but the tribe's rules of witchcraft exorcism did not permit them to kill him at once. Rather, they had to torture him to death. However, in order for Chief Yakesha to recover, it was necessary that the boy die within 10 days.

Once Kodik was warm and had a bit of food, he told

them a horrible story. To lessen his "evil" powers, the elders had kicked his head. Then they had starved him, beat him and jabbed his chest with sharp-pointed sticks. They had tied his hands behind his back, scalded him with steam from a boiling kettle and finally thrust him into the icy hole in the porch and left him to freeze to death.

Constable Leeson knew the Chilcat elders would soon discover that the boy had been rescued and would come looking for him. He also expected the Chilcat to take reprisals while the NWMP constables stayed at the mission. But when nothing happened, he sent the other two officers back across the Canadian border to the Wells detachment.

No sooner had the two men left than the angry Chilcat elders surrounded the mission and demanded the return of Kodik, the "wizard." One of the chiefs, Yiltock, led a group intent on killing Mr. Sellon, but the chief stopped short when he recognized that the man standing beside the missionary with his gun drawn was actually the out-of-uniform Canadian Mountie, Constable Leeson. Yiltock explained to Leeson that witchcraft was killing his people, and that in order to stop the evil, he needed Kodik returned to him. Leeson refused.

The Chilcat continued to surround the house throughout the night, but at dawn they disappeared. When Constable Brown arrived around noon to check on Leeson's safety, he reported that most of the people in the village were sleeping. Quickly, the officers bundled up the boy and smuggled him past the village, across the border and into the safety of their police detachment. Kodik stayed with the NWMP there until he received safe refuge in the Alaska Industrial School at Sitka.

Mounties in Siberia

In May 1919, when six RNWMP officers and 154 of their horses boarded the train in eastern Siberia to travel 6,000 kilometres across war-torn Russia, they were about to experience one of the most unusual episodes in Mountie history.

At the time, the First World War was over but Russia was in the midst of a bitter civil war between its new Soviet government, which had gained power after the Bolshevik Revolution in October 1917, and the anti-Bolshevik White Russians, who were trying to regain control.

Back in July of 1918, the Allied countries of the First World War had agreed to help the White Russians by sending in an international force. On August 12, 1918, Canada became a part of that Allied commitment—and the Russian Civil War—when the Canadian government formed an expeditionary force for Siberia, including an RNWMP cavalry unit, known as Squadron B, Siberia, of 190 men and 181 police horses. Over half the squadron were veteran police officers from detachments, while the remainder consisted of young men in their late teens from the Prairies. The well-trained horses were from ranches in Alberta and Saskatchewan, and many had served with the Mounties for years.

A 20-man advance RNWMP party, consisting of one officer and 20 other ranks, sailed to Vladivostok in early October. The rest of the men, plus the horses, left Vancouver on November 17 onboard the SS *Monteagle*. Before the second group even set sail, the war in Europe had come to an end; the Armistice had been signed on November 11—but the RNMWP squadron left anyway.

By 1919, the eastern Siberia port city of Vladivostok was full of Allied troops whose job it was to stop the region from falling to the Bolsheviks and to keep the Trans-Siberian Railroad open to transport Allied supplies to the Whites.

The Mounties didn't see any action in Siberia. Rather, they spent the next several months carrying out routine duties in the Vladivostok region. In April 1919, the Canadian forces began to withdraw from Siberia. Though the men were happy to go home, there was a downside: the Mountie horses of Squadron B would not be returning with them. Instead, they were to be delivered to the White Russians fighting at Yekaterinburg in the Ural Mountains. This meant the animals would have to endure a long and dangerous train journey of 6,400 kilometres.

On May 17, 1919, the horses were reluctantly moved from the RNWMP barracks to the railway yard outside Vladivostok. It was difficult for the Mounties to say goodbye to their horses—many of the men had served for some time with the same horse back in Canada. Because the long train journey required experienced horsemen to look after the animals, six Mounties volunteered their services; the remainder of Squadron B prepared to sail back to Canada.

The next day (May 18), the trainload of horses pulled out of the station with Sergeant J.E. "Teddy" Margetts in charge of the volunteer RNWMP brigade. As they railed towards Yekaterinburg through North China, frequent stops were made so that the brigade could give the horses fresh water and exercise. Nevertheless, some of the horses became ill.

Two weeks later, on June 4, the six Mounties found themselves fighting in Russia's civil war, west of Lake Baikal near the remote Siberian town of Tayshet. The Bolsheviks attacked the train, derailing it on a steep embankment. Boxcars were overturned, and 19 of them were "smashed to atoms." Two Russian guards and 15 RNWMP horses were killed, and 24 Russian soldiers were injured.

The scene was a disaster. Many horses were trapped inside the overturned boxcars, while others lay in the wreckage, so badly injured that they had to be destroyed. Sergeant Margetts, with the assistance of the Russians, quickly took charge of the rescue operation, his actions enabling the trapped animals to be rescued.

In the confusion, 20 to 30 horses had bolted from the overturned cars and galloped away in a frightened frenzy. The Mounties refused to abandon the animals in the Siberian wilderness, so four members—led by Corporal Philip Bossard—quickly mounted and went after the fleeing horses. They risked sniper fire and capture by the retreating Reds as they rode several kilometres into the countryside, determined to bring every fleeing horse back to the train. Incredibly, they were successful in their goal.

Several days later, the train resumed its journey and arrived at Yekaterinburg on June 25, 1919. After handing over the horses to the White Russians, the Mounties headed back to Vladivostok and took a steamer home to Canada.

The 1919 Siberian trek was one of the longest journeys ever made by a trainload of military horses. A few days after they received the animals, the Whites retreated and the city was captured by the Bolsheviks. In October of 1919, four months later, the Russian Civil War was over and the new Soviet Bolshevik government was firmly in power. The fate of the Mountie horses, however, is unknown.

Both Margetts and Brossard were decorated for their leadership and action during the derailment. Margetts received the Meritorious Service Medal and Bossard the Military Medal for "Gallantry and Distinguished Service." The participation of the RNWMP in the Russian Civil War is recognized on the Force's guidon: "Siberia 1918-19."

Rumrunning Patrols

The first Mountie water patrol took place in 1890 on Lake Winnipeg, with the sailing vessel *Keewatin* attempting to control the illegal liquor trade. Sadly, the *Keewatin* met with tragedy a few months later. The rough waters of a sudden storm caused the three-man boat to overturn on September 7. Two men, Corporal Harry Olive Morphy and Constable G.Q.R. de Beaujeau, climbed up the side of the boat and held on until the next day, when, fatigued, they let go and drowned. The sailing master, 66-year-old Captain Watts, survived the initial accident by clinging to the wreck for days before being rescued. He was rushed to a Winnipeg hospital where he told his story but then died from his injuries.

Though an RCMP Marine Division was not officially formed until 1932, water patrols had continued since those early days of the *Keewatin*, and sea-going Mounties were already calling themselves "saltwater cowboys and horse marines."

Fifty years after the original NWMP put an end to illegal whisky trading on the Prairies, the Mounties had another liquor problem to deal with. This time it was illicit liquor smuggling—better known as rumrunning—on the Canadian East Coast. Government officials saw rumrunning as one of the most pressing national problems, and they tasked the RCMP to bring about its elimination.

By the 1920s, the United States and many Canadian provinces had passed legislation to prohibit the sale and consumption of alcoholic beverages. As a result, rumrunning became a somewhat "respected" occupation in Atlantic Canada. Many families made good money with their fleets of rumrunning boats, and some of the best fishing captains were rumoured to be rumrunners.

Vessels were either specially built or adapted to transport the cargo from main pickup places like the French-owned St. Pierre and Miquelon Islands in the Gulf of St. Lawrence. Most of the illegal liquor was produced in Montreal and Toronto.

The RCMP was kept busy. In one year, they carried out over 400 rumrunning patrols. One of the most sensational of these cases took place off the coast of Nova Scotia in July 1923, when the rum-smuggling schooner *Veda M. McKeown* was intercepted at sea.

On the night of July 3, Detective-Sergeant J.P. Blakeney, Corporal W.A. Caldwell and Constable F.P. Fahey dressed in plain clothes and set out to sea in a motorboat in search of the *Veda M. McKeown*. They soon sighted the schooner, which was anchored offshore and waiting for buyers to come and purchase liquor onboard. The RCMP flashed the special recognition signal to show the captain and eight crew members that they had come to buy liquor, and then steered the police boat alongside the schooner.

Pretending to be a buyer, Blakeney climbed aboard the ship. He haggled with the captain over the price of whisky, rum and gin until they settled on a number. Blakeney then watched as the liquor was transferred to the RMCP boat. However, after two 10-gallon kegs of rum were passed from the schooner to Caldwell and Fahie in the motorboat, the captain suddenly halted the transfer.

He explained that until he got the cash, he would not

hand over another keg of rum. Blakeney listened and then said, "Just a moment. I'm a sergeant of the Royal Canadian Mounted Police and I'm also a Customs and Excise officer. In the name of the King, I arrest you and your crew, and I'm seizing your ship and cargo." While he was talking, Caldwell and Fahie sprang onboard and took up the prearranged strategic positions on the boat.

The fast turn of events had caught the rumrunners by surprise. Everyone was dead silent. The rumrunners were calculating their chances of escape. A minute or so went by, and still no one spoke. Then, suddenly, shouts and threats were hurled at the Mounties, but they stood firm, prepared to use force if necessary.

Begrudgingly, the captain and crew surrendered and were later prosecuted. The next day, under orders from Blakeney, the *Veda M. McKeown*, with a cargo of nearly 2,000 gallons of rum, 200 cases of Scotch whisky and 34 cases of gin, sailed into port.

Even 40 years after their first liquor arrest in 1873, the Mounties were keeping up their tradition of smashing the illegal liquor trade.

Medical Emergency

While controlling rumrunners was pulling the RCMP to the edge of Canada's legal boundary, another kind of boundary breaking—one of a more personal nature—was taking place in the Arctic, where a 30-year-old Mountie, Constable Henry

Stallworthy, was forced by circumstance to perform a task beyond anything he could have ever imagined.

In 1923, Stallworthy, who already had nine years of RCMP service under his belt, was stationed at the Chesterfield Inlet detachment. A year later, he was joined at the Arctic post by Staff Sergeant S.G. Clay and his 33-year-old wife Margaret, or "Maggie," one of the few white women in the Arctic. This was not Maggie's first time in the North—she had already lived in the Mackenzie River area during her husband's last posting.

Shortly after they arrived at Chesterfield Inlet, Staff Sergeant Clay was invited to join the HBC traders on their fall patrol up the Back River to Baker Lake–Thelon District. Maggie encouraged her husband to go and get to know the area and perhaps meet some of the Native people. His absence wouldn't bother her—she was used to spending many hours alone while her husband was on patrol. Besides, she was happy to stay and learn about her new community, where, unfortunately, too many loose dogs roamed.

Maggie liked to walk along the beach, where children often played. It was on a September afternoon when Constable Stallworthy, on duty with Corporal O.G. Petty, first heard a dogfight on the beach and then heard Maggie scream. Both men stormed out of their post and were greeted by a horrible scene. Maggie was lying on the ground surrounded by snarling dogs that had torn the flesh from her knee to her ankle, leaving the bare bone exposed. The men chased the dogs away, then picked Maggie up carefully and carried her back up the slope to her home.

Stallworthy worked with two HBC men and two Roman Catholic priests to stop further blood loss and make Maggie as comfortable as possible. But Maggie was in terrible pain and begged the men to amputate her leg. Suspecting they had no choice but to amputate, the men agreed that they would perform the procedure the following morning. However, none of them had experienced this kind of medical emergency before. They were equipped with only the most basic surgical tools and supplies and a very small amount of chloroform for anaesthetic. Antibiotics had not yet been developed, so every surgery carried the additional risk of infection.

The men assigned each other tasks for the operation: Father Duplesne would perform the surgery; the HBC's trading-post manager, Norman Snow, would assist him; Petty and Stallworthy would look after the surgical instruments and dressing; and, during the surgery, Stallworthy would administer the anaesthetic. The only medical text at the inlet was *Pye's Surgery*, and the men spent the night studying the book. There was no way to call for outside medical assistance—the group was on its own.

Everyone present, including Maggie, signed a pre-surgery statement: "We believe that the amputation of Mrs. Clay's leg is necessary. We have every reason to believe that we can succeed. We believe that this will save her life."

The dining room table became the operating table. Stallworthy lifted Maggie onto the table and administered the chloroform. When he felt it had taken effect, he signalled Father Duplesne to begin the surgery. But when it came time for the priest to begin sawing through the bone, he couldn't do it. Constable Stallworthy quickly took over, handing the chloroform to the post's Inuit interpreter, Maria. He finished amputating the leg just as the effects of the chloroform wore off.

Awake when Stallworthy carried her to her bed, Maggie asked, "Is my leg off? I feel so much better." A little later she asked, "I won't be able to dance again, will I?"

Initially, everyone was optimistic that Maggie would recover. However, the shock and blood loss were too great and her condition quickly deteriorated. When the two priests tried to convert her to Roman Catholicism so they could administer the last sacrament, she became so upset that she asked Stallworthy to stay beside her to give her the strength to say no.

Maggie knew she was dying and would never see her husband again, so she had Stallworthy write down her thoughts and messages to her husband. The constable comforted her and gave her sips of tea. About midnight of the third day, she died.

The men made her a rudimentary coffin, and Maria lined it with duffel and fine white cloth. Then, after an Anglican memorial service read from the prayer book,

Maggie was buried on the barren hill behind the detachment, and a rock cairn was built to cover the coffin.

A few weeks later, her husband returned with the HBC schooner. Stallworthy met the boat. Immediately sensing that something was terribly wrong, Staff Sergeant Clay shouted, "Where is Maggie?" When Stallworthy told him of her death, he was devastated.

The following spring, both Stallworthy and Clay left Chesterfield Inlet and travelled to the Niagara Peninsula to bring the tragic news to Maggie's family. Clay took discharge and never returned to the Force. Stallworthy transferred to the Jasper detachment after a brief visit to England and was later stationed at Bache Peninsula on Ellesmere Island. He became one of Canada's greatest Arctic travellers.

The Incredible Sea Saga of the *St. Roch*

Throughout the 1920s, the RCMP continued to push northern boundaries, establishing police posts throughout the Yukon, the Northwest Territories and the Arctic Archipelago. In 1927, the Force decided to get its own patrol vessel for Arctic supply service. The ship would also serve as a floating detachment in the summer and a stationary one in the winter.

A small schooner named *St. Roch* was launched on May 7, 1928, to do the job. By the time it was retired 26 years later, the *St. Roch* had become a seafaring legend, along with its captain, Staff Sergeant Henry A. Larsen.

In 1903, after more than 400 years of failed attempts by other sailors and ships, Norwegian explorer Roald Amundsen began the successful navigation of his small ship *Gjoa* through the elusive Northwest Passage. It took the explorer three years (1903–06) to journey from the Atlantic Ocean, across the top of North America, to the Pacific Ocean. Despite this success, it would be many more years before a vessel would sail the passage from west to east, or travel it both ways. The accomplishment of both these feats was set in motion in 1940—the year the *St. Roch* was sent on a secret wartime mission and ended up making seafaring history.

Built in Vancouver during the winter of 1927–28, the *St. Roch* was 32 metres long with an 8-metre beam and a 150 horsepower Union Diesel Engine supplemented with an 18 horsepower auxiliary diesel engine. She was constructed of a combination of Douglas fir and Australian gumwood—the only wood known to withstand the grinding effects of ice pressure. Her spartan quarters were cramped, and she was by no means a pretty ship—Larsen called her "Ugly Duckling."

From 1928 to 1940, the *St. Roch* plied the western Arctic waters from her home port of Vancouver to the Mackenzie River, often spending long Arctic winters frozen in the ice.

By the spring of 1940, the Second World War was underway, and all RCMP boats, like other Canadian vessels, were put under naval war command. Larsen was just getting ready to leave Vancouver in June for his annual winter patrol when he received a rather strange order: he was to set out for Greenland on a secret mission to secure bauxite and cryolite mines—crucial for the Allies' wartime aluminum production. The *St. Roch* was to meet the military on Labrador's north coast and proceed to Greenland to secure the mines.

Larsen knew it would be an extremely difficult task to accomplish. To get to Greenland, the little ship first had to sail east through the dangerous, unpredictable waters of the Northwest Passage. But if anyone could do it, it was Larsen, Canada's most experienced Arctic navigator and an expert on Arctic expeditions.

Born in Fredrikstad, Norway, in 1899, Larsen had been at sea since the age of 15. He had joined the RCMP in 1928 as the first mate aboard the newly launched *St. Roch*. By the end of that year, he had been appointed skipper and, for the next 20 years, had taken the *St. Roch* on its annual Arctic patrols. Larsen admired the Inuit for their ability to survive in a harsh environment, and he was sensitive to their culture. They taught him to handle a dog team and hunt seal, and they affectionately called him *Hanorie Umiarjuag* (or *Umiarpolik*), meaning "Henry with the Big Ship."

On June 21, 1940, the *St. Roch* left Vancouver on its historic voyage, with Larsen and a crew of eight. From the beginning, things did not go smoothly. A few days after setting sail, engine trouble forced them to stop and make repairs to the deck machinery. Two weeks later, when she entered the Bering Sea, the *St. Roch* ran into violent winds and rain that lasted all day and night. When the gales subsided, the vessel continued to the American Pacific whaling station wharf at Akutan Harbour, where deckhands P.G. Hunt and Albert J. Chartrand filled the freshwater tanks before the crew sailed out again.

On July 22, they saw just a scattering of sea ice, but soon there was more. It got thicker and thicker until, on July 24, they were forced to cut the engines and let the *St. Roch* drift with the ice pack. By August 2, she was working eastward, mooring to ice floes when the ice got too heavy. Five days later, within sight of the Cross Islands, the *St. Roch* became sandwiched in the floes and was unable to move until August 10, when the ice gave way (with some additional help from blasting powder) and the vessel got to open water.

After 70 days at sea, the *St. Roch* arrived at Herschel Island on August 11, and just over a month later, on September 16, the crew reached Cambridge Bay, where they took on dogs for their winter patrols. It had been a rough journey, battling bad weather, strong winds and ice, but the *St. Roch* was accustomed to this sort of harrowing autumn travel in the western Arctic, just before she froze in for the winter.

Larsen had not planned to overwinter on this particular voyage because the *St. Roch* was to continue to Greenland, but the weather worked against them and Larsen knew it was now too late to attempt to complete the journey. The *St. Roch* would have to winter in the frozen ice.

Larsen had two choices: he and his crew could either winter at Banks Island or Walker Bay. Banks Island was a well-protected harbour—an ideal spot for winter quarters. But when they arrived there, something didn't look right to Larsen. The high mounds of rock and pushed-up gravel meant there had been heavy ice pressure in the spring, and Larsen knew that could be deadly to the *St. Roch*. The captain decided to leave Banks Island and chance the unpredictable Arctic weather to sail over to Walker Bay on the west coast of Victoria Island.

The *St. Roch* arrived safely at the bay on October 5 and chose a wintering site about 270 metres from shore. Quickly the crew unloaded the fuel oil, coal and boats onto the beach and before the bay was frozen on October 30 the *St. Roch* was encased in its winter home under a canvas-covered wooden frame. The crew settled in for the long, dark winter, doing the work they normally did while overwintering. This included dogsled patrolling, preventing incursions by foreign hunters and whalers, visiting the scattered Inuit camps, recording weather, enforcing game laws and more.

For 10 months, the *St. Roch* remained frozen in the ice at Walker Bay. It wasn't until July 31, 1941, that she sailed out of her winter quarters. After stopping at Holman Island to investigate the accidental shooting of an Inuit boy, the ship ran into heavy scattered ice and thick wet fog. She inched along, stopping and mooring to ice floes to avoid danger. On August 2, she anchored off Cape Bathhurst in deep fog. Later, when she sailed on, she almost foundered in fierce gales that lasted a few days.

For the next month, the *St. Roch* encountered extreme weather conditions and sometimes had to take shelter for days at a time. Larsen continued to sail eastward in a strong current, passed Booth Point and dropped anchor at Gjoa Haven. When snow and hail forced the men and their ship to seek shelter in the lee of Mount Matheson, a strong northwest gale tossed and rolled the vessel "like a cork."

On September 1, there was more trouble for the *St. Roch*: she was faced with a solid pack of ice in a very strong current. Larsen anchored the vessel on a grounded floe, but soon the ice began to close in on her. That night, while a heavy snowstorm raged, great ice chunks struck the ship. Thankfully her two anchors held, and the next morning the wind changed, blowing the ice chunks away from the ship. Throughout the day, the *St. Roch* inched along, anchoring close to shore while trying to find decent shelter from the incoming ice. But that night, when the vessel was in the open again, another violent snowstorm hit, completely covering the ice and shoreline.

On September 3, Larsen sighted and entered Pasley Bay, an inlet on the Boothia Peninsula. The next day, on a trip to shore, the crew saw that the ice had pushed up against the coast, totally blocking the inlet entrance. Now completely surrounded by ice, the ship was being forced further down the bay by the pressure of the ice, and she was powerless to stop it. When the ice movement briefly decreased, the *St. Roch* headed for a patch of open water and anchored. But that night, strong winds pushed the floes up to the vessel and, once again, she was locked in heavy ice.

The ship was helpless when on September 6 she struck a shoal, pivoted twice, and listed to port and then to starboard. But luckily, the continued ice pressure pushed her over the shoal with 7 feet of water, dragging her anchors and 90 fathoms of chain. She was again afloat, moving and shifting with the ice, until she jammed close to the beach.

By September 11, 1941, the whole inlet was frozen solid and there was no escape for the *St. Roch*—she had to winter there. By the end of September, some gear and 15 tons of coal were taken off the ship and piled on the ice, and the winter housing was erected over the vessel.

A long but busy season lay ahead. Among the many treks made that winter was a 61-day patrol by Larsen and Hunt. Needing to take an Inuit census of the vast area, the two men travelled over 1,700 kilometres in weather never milder than –48°C.

It was also a winter of tragedy. On February 13, 1942, Constable Albert Joseph Chartrand suffered a heart attack and died within a few minutes. The crew buried him at Pasley Bay and erected a stone cairn and cross to mark his gravesite.

On August 3, 1942, after 11 months at Pasley Bay, the *St. Roch* worked her way out about 25 kilometres north before meeting ice with one narrow lead extending a few kilometres west. Larsen decided to see if the ice would break, but it didn't—the lead closed and the *St. Roch* was again a prisoner of the ice.

It was a frightening wait. At times, severe ice pressure lifted the vessel up as high as four feet, heeling her over from side to side. The crew set charges of black powder close to the ship to relieve the pressure, cracking the ice to form a cushion around her. Back and forth she drifted, perilously close to destruction. Several times, even Larsen felt the vessel was doomed. Adding to their problems, a cylinder head broke on August 12, causing the main engine to flood and leaving the *St. Roch* with only five cylinders to operate.

On August 24, a strong northerly gale opened up the ice, and the ship sailed to safe anchorage in deep water between the Tasmania Islands. Slowly the vessel made her way through the passage as Larsen worked the tide, dodged icebergs and battled strong currents and jammed ice.

On September 6, the *St. Roch* arrived at Pond Inlet, took on some fuel and then sailed into the infamous iceberg-strewn Davis Strait, battling strong southeast gales, violent squalls and mounting swells. But Larsen pushed through the bad weather and poor visibility, past Baffin Island and down the coast of Labrador.

On September 30, the *St. Roch* reached Corner Brook,

Newfoundland. On October 8, she reached Sydney Harbour, Cape Breton Island. And on October 11, at 3:30 p.m., after having travelled over 15,000 kilometres and spending 819 days at sea, the little RCMP patrol boat arrived at Halifax. Though the secret mission was never accomplished, the *St. Roch* broke boundaries by becoming the second ship to successfully navigate the Northwest Passage and the first to do so from west to east.

The *St. Roch* and Larsen worked on the East Coast until 1944, when they once again sailed the passage, this time from east to west. They followed a new route (via Lancaster, Viscount and Melville Sounds and Prince of Wales Strait) and completed the journey in three months (July 16 to October 16), making history as the first ship to navigate the passage both ways.

But she wasn't finished making history. In the early 1950s, she became the first ship to circumnavigate North America twice, via the Panama Canal. When she returned to Vancouver in 1954, the City of Vancouver purchased the *St. Roch*, towed her to Kits Point and brought her ashore in 1958. Four years later, in 1962, the *St. Roch* was declared a National Historic Site and is now on permanent display at the Vancouver Maritime Museum.

Larsen left the *St. Roch* before 1950, but remained with the RCMP as a superintendent until his retirement in 1961 with 33 years of service. Larsen Sound (between James Ross Strait and Franklin Strait) and Larsen Inlet are named for him.

Epilogue

IN THE RNWMP CORPS HISTORY of 1906, Captain Ernest J. Chambers wrote about a young constable who had become lost on patrol during a severe winter blizzard. Before he died, the young Mountie had scrawled these few brief sentences: "Lost, horse dead. Am trying to push ahead. Have done my best." Chambers commented on the honour and sense of duty of the "gallant member of this remarkable force of soldier-police" and added a tribute, one that is still fitting for the women and men of today's RCMP:

> That has always been the spirit of the Royal North-West Mounted Police, and wherever the duty of the force is to lie in the future, these capable officers and dashing, daring men may be depended upon to do their best, and to add many chapters just as honourable as to those preceding them to the chivalrous, romantic and patriotic record of the force.

Bibliography

Anderson, Frank W. *The Death of Albert Johnson*. Calgary: Frontier Publishing Ltd., 1968.

Anderson, Frank W. *Fort Walsh and The Cypress Hills*. Humbolt, Saskatchewan: Gopher Books, 1999.

Berton, Pierre. *Klondike, The Last Great Gold Rush 1896–1899*. Toronto: McClelland & Stewart, Inc., 1997.

Chambers, Ernest J. *The Royal North-West Mounted Police, A Corps History*. Montreal: Mortimer Press, 1906. Reprint, Toronto: Coles Publishing Company, 1973.

Dempsey, Hugh A., ed. *Men in Scarlet*. Calgary: Historical Society of Alberta/McClelland and Stewart West, 1974.

Dempsey, Hugh A. *William Parker, Mounted Policeman*. Edmonton: Hurtig Publishers, 1973.

Evans, R.G. *Murder on the Frontier*. Surrey: Heritage House Publishing Company Ltd., 1980.

Fetherstonhaugh, R.C. *The Royal Canadian Mounted Police*. New York: Garden City Publishing Co. Inc., 1940.

Kelly, Nora and William. *The Royal Canadian Mounted Police, A Century of History*. Edmonton: Hurtig Publishers, 1973.

Kelly, William H. *The Mounties As They Saw Themselves*. Ottawa: The Golden Dog Press. 1996.

Kemp, Vernon A.M. *Scarlet and Stetson, The Royal North-West Mounted Police on the Prairies*. Toronto: The Ryerson Press, 1964.

Kuhn, Edgar A. *Ellesmere Land: A Mountie in the High Arctic*. Weyburn, Saskatchewan: Edgar A. Kuhn, 2002.

Lotz, Jim. *The Mounties: The History of the Royal Canadian Mounted Police*. Greenwich: Bison Books, 1984.

Macpherson, M.A. *Outlaws of the Canadian West*. Edmonton: Lone Pine Publishing, 1999.

Manzione, Joseph. *I Am Looking To The North For My Life. Sitting Bull 1876–1881*. Salt Lake City: University of Utah Press, 1994.

Nicol, Eric, ed. *Dickens of the Mounted*. Toronto: McClelland & Stewart Inc., 1989.

North, Dick. *The Lost Patrol*. Anchorage: Alaska Northwest Publishing Company, 1978.

Price, Ray. *The Howling Arctic*. Toronto: Peter Martin Associates, 1974.

Steele, S.B. *Forty Years in Canada. Reminiscences of the Great North-West with Some Account of His Service in South Africa*. New York: Dodd, Mead & Co., 1915. Reprint, Toronto: Prospero Books, 2000.

Stenson, Fred. *RCMP: The March West*. Nepean: GAPC Entertainment Inc., 1999.

Weir, John. *Back Door to the Klondike*. Erin: The Boston Mills Press, 1988.

Young, Delbert A. *The Mounties*. Don Mills: PaperJacks, 1973.

Index

Acknowledgements

Researching this book has introduced me, through print, to amazing Mountie policing pioneers. Some have become legends, while many others reside quietly in the historical records. Thank you to all of them for their courage and dedication to duty in often difficult and dangerous environments.

Special thanks to Daryl Demoskoff and Nadine Howard of Tourism Saskatchewan, who arranged for me to visit the Royal Canadian Mounted Police Museum while I was on a trip to Regina. The tour was inspiring and led to the writing of this book on the Mounties.

Big thanks to my husband, Glenn, for making sure I always had fresh coffee or tea and a home-cooked meal while I was immersed in completing the book. And thank you to my children—Tania, Tami and Cindi—for their suggestions, comments and enthusiastic support while I was researching and writing the book.

Accolades also to my editor, Lesley Reynolds, for her excellent suggestions and editing skills in fine-tuning the book, and to Heritage House Publishing for getting the book to print and the market.

About the Author

Elle Andra-Warner is an author, journalist and photographer based in Thunder Bay, Ontario. She specializes in writing about history, culture, travel, people and business and is the bestselling author of books about Canadian history, including *Hudson's Bay Company Adventures: Tales of Canada's Fur Traders*, also published by Heritage House. Her award-winning articles appear regularly in major publications, and her regular newspaper columns on business, travel and history have been in print since 1994. As a corporate writer, her list of clients includes municipalities, corporations, travel associations and arts organizations.

A political studies graduate of Lakehead University, Elle is a member of the Professional Writers of Canada, Travel Media of Canada, the Writers Union of Canada and the Writers Guild of Alberta. She has given journalism workshops throughout Canada, is an online guest journalism lecturer for UCLA (University of California, Los Angeles), and is the co-editor of the Thunder Bay Historical Museum Society's annual journal, *Papers & Records*.

Estonian by heritage, Elle was born in a post–Second World War United Nations displaced persons camp for Estonians in Eckernforde, West Germany. She came to Canada with her parents, settling in Port Arthur, Ontario (now the city of Thunder Bay). Except for 2001–2004, when she lived in the Northwest Territories and Alberta, Thunder Bay has been Elle's home since her arrival in Canada.